# F**OO**D
# SPIRITS

# FOOD & SPIRITS

## Stories by Beth Brant

### (*Degonwadonti*)

Firebrand
Books

Several of the stories in this collection have appeared previously in the following books and magazines: *All My Relations* edited by Thomas King (Canadian Alliance in Solidarity with Native Peoples, 1988), *The American Voice, Canadian Fiction Magazine, Ikon, Making Face, Making Soul/Haciendo Caras* edited by Gloria Anzaldúa (Aunt Lute Foundation, 1990), and *Tiger Lily*.

Book and cover design by Betsy Bayley
Typesetting by Bets Ltd.

Printed on acid-free paper in the United States by McNaughton & Gunn

Library of Congress Cataloging-in-Publication Data

Brant, Beth, 1941–
    Food & spirits : stories / by Beth Brant (Degonwadonti).
        p.    cm.
    ISBN 0-932379-93-1 (cloth) — ISBN 0-932379-92-3 (paper)
    1. Mohawk Indians—Fiction.    I. Title.    II. Title: Food and
    spirits.
PR9199.3.B6878F6    1991
813'.54—dc20                                              91-10343
                                                              CIP

# Acknowledgments

I want to thank every Indian woman and man who has crossed my path since the publication of my last book. You have given me strength, given me beauty. I remember each one of you.

Dr. Sarah Jessup, true sister and healer, I thank you for pulling me through a long, debilitating illness without thinking how you were going to be paid. This book is the result of that healing.

Michelle Cliff, who has always been there for me, I thank you with love and gratitude.

Kim, Jennifer, and Jill, my dear daughters, I thank you for being my allies, my friends, my support in times of despair and triumph.

Nathanael, Benjamin, and Zachary, my beloved grandsons, I thank you for giving me another way to view the world through your beautiful innocent eyes.

I thank Denise Dorsz, loving friend for fourteen years, who has inspired and challenged me, made communion with me, listened to the corn, who shared an Island with me—who brought forth the Blue Heron.

I thank the Mother Of All Things, who has sent blessings and lessons, who has sent many signs to bring me comfort and solace, who sent Eagle with the gift of beading words together to make writing. Who has given me life.

# Contents

*This book is for Denise.*

*I expect almost everything*
*from words*
*not even knowing*
*what they promise*
*or deny me,*
*what lies beyond*
*the echo they strike.*
*I do not know*
*whether they are born on my lips*
*or whether someone is prompting me*
*in a mute language*
*whose code I cannot crack.*

Alaíde Foppa
Translated by Rozenn Frère and Dennis Nurske


*I have written down my faith.*

Emile Nelligan

# Preface

# Telling

*for Celeste who told me to tell
and for Vickie*

Her face is wide, innocent, clear.
She tells me things.
They are secrets. "He did this to me. He told me not to tell. I never
told until now."
Her face twists for an instant, then returns to its rightful beauty.
I listen.
She doesn't cry, but my eyes feel the familiar moisture seeping out,
dropping on my hand that holds hers. How dare these tears appear
when she—who has the courage to tell—doesn't weep.
She gives me this.
Secrets.

I receive a package in the mail.
When I open it, a diary falls into my hands.
How she got my name, my address, she doesn't say.
Her letter says: *I needed to show this to you. You can throw the di-
ary away if you want. I just needed to tell.*
The diary is pink. There are gold words stamped on the cover—
*Dear Diary.*
I am afraid to open you, *Dear Diary.*

Afraid of the secrets I have to keep.
*He did this to me. My father did this to me. They did this to me. They did this.*
I think the pages should weep as I do when I read her life.
Who turned away from her need to tell?
Who could throw away the pink vinyl book of a life, a life thrown away by others? By others' need to throw away a life?
What do I do with this, *Dear Diary?*
A writer can read. She can hear. She can write.
What does she do with the need of someone to tell?

Our foster child comes to live with us.
One leg is crippled, the burn marks shriveling the skin.
This is his fifth foster home. He is three years old. He is difficult.
He burns with anger—the scars we cannot see.
He can't talk. He points to things and grunts. In three years, has no one noticed he can't speak words?
My anger burns me. I feel as if I have swallowed hot grease.
What does *his* anger feel like?
We enroll him in a preschool for a few hours of the day, hoping the exchange with other children will help him heal. I take him to school and explain that he will be playing with other kids for a while and I will be back to get him.
When I return, he comes out into the hall, a look of surprise on his little, dark face.
He smiles with delight at me.
I realize he thought I wasn't coming back.
And he accepted it as normal, as right.
My precious throwaway boy.
We taught you how to talk.
You were innocent. You were difficult.
Innocent.

I write.
I wonder what difference it makes. This writing, this scribble on

paper.

The secrets I am told grow in my stomach. They make me want to vomit. They stay in me and my stomach twists—like her lovely face—and my hands reach for a pen, a typewriter to calm the rage and violence that make a home in me.

I write.

I sit in this room away from my own, yellow legal pad beneath my hand, pen gripped tightly in my fingers. The writer who no longer writes directly on paper. The writer who uses machines to say the words.

This pen feels like a knife in my hand.

The paper should bleed, like my peoples' bodies.


I have a dream about Betty Osborne.

The last secrets of her life.

Stabbed fifty-six times with a screwdriver to keep the secrets of whitemen.

Betty, your crime was being a woman, an Indian. Your punishment, mutilation and death.

The town kept the secret of who killed you.

Seventeen years before the names were said out loud.

They keep secrets to protect whitemen.

Who do I protect with the secrets given me?

My pen is a knife.

I carve the letters B E T T Y  O S B O R N E on this yellow page.

Surely the paper must bleed from your name.

Why doesn't it bleed for you, my throwaway sister?

The sister I never met except in my dream, my obscene nightmare.

Betty, do I betray you by writing your name for people to see who will not love you?

*What good is a poet. . .* Chrystos

From "I Dreamt Again Tonight of That Beach" by Chrystos in *Not Vanishing* (Press Gang, 1988).

I think about those words today and they hang like a knife—or a screwdriver—over my head, ready to pierce me and render me speechless.

My speech that reveals itself on paper.

*What good is a poet?*

What good is this pen, this yellow paper, if I can't fashion them into tools or weapons to change our lives?

How do I use this weapon when I must hold the secrets safe?

This is not safe—being a writer.

*We are the paint for their palette.*\* Salli Benedict

What kind of picture is painted with the ink I commit to this paper?

How will they use it against us?

Will I be the same as them?

I love. They do not.

Will love make the difference?

Today I woke bleeding from my vagina.

My menses ended days ago.

Is this where the blood goes?

Running out of my womb instead of onto the page, into the words, the weapon.

The words.

Ugly words.

RAPE. MURDER. TORTURE. SPEECHLESSNESS.

I write and make words that are not beautiful.

RAPE. MURDER. TORTURE. SPEECHLESSNESS.

*Dear Diary,* did you give her what she needs?

Do I give her what she needs?

A friend. A secret-keeper.

Love.

From a presentation given by Salli Benedict at the American Studies Conference held in Toronto, Canada, in November 1989.

If love could be made visible, something to hold in the hand, would it be this pen, this weapon, these words I cannot stop writing?
What were Betty's words?
Where did our foster child's words go?
Do words disappear, or do they linger behind like ghosts?
Do they float like spirits?
Do they cut through to a place I can barely imagine?
When I expose words, who do I betray?

*If you hide the stories in the bureau drawer, they become Bad Medicine.** Maria Campbell

Are some stories meant to be hidden?
What we do to each other.
What we do between us. The secret, ugly things we do to each other.
How do I show the blood of them? The ink of our own palette?
Medicine.
Who will heal the writer who uses her ink and blood to tell?
Telling.
Who hears?

Our foster child is with us one year. In that time he speaks, he cries, he points to his leg and asks, "What happened? Who did this?"
A judge gives him back to his mother, the same mother they say burned him.
And I wonder if the mother has kept a secret of her own.
Her man's secret.
Has she lost her child for three years because of another's secret?
What lengths and depths do we go to to protect our own?
The depth of losing a child.
The length of being branded as the torturer of an infant.
Secrets to protect.
These pages should bleed.

Conversation with the author.

*Dear Diary,* did you give her what she needs?

Can I give what she needs?

Medicine.

I want my words to be Medicine.

Will the same Medicine heal the writer who carries these stories inside her like knives?

*He did this to me.*

*They did this to me.*

I believe her.

Does she tell me so *I* can tell? The me that shapes words into weapons.

What can heal the writer who dreams of Betty Osborne and can only imagine her words?

Her last words. *NO. NO. NO.*

What can heal the writer who struggles to say the words for a little boy? A child who cannot speak until he has been loved.

*Dear Diary,* did your blank pages absorb the shock of the words written on you?

*Dear Diary,* did you give her what she needs?

The need to tell and be believed.


I need to tell.

Carving letters on yellow paper to understand the violence committed against us, by us.

What can heal the writer who feels the screwdriver in her dreams?

Who can heal the writer that feels the burning of a child's leg?

What will heal the writer who feels like a traitor as she writes these words, this language of our enemy, on these yellow pages?

She said to me: "I need to tell you this. You will believe me."

She wrote: *You can throw away this diary, but I needed you to know.*

He said to me, pointing to his leg, "Who did this?"

*We* did this.

And *they* told us to be speechless.

But they taught us new words that do not exist in our own language.

RAPE. MURDER. TORTURE. SPEECHLESSNESS. INCEST.

POVERTY. ADDICTION.

These obscene words that do not appear in our own language.

What good is a poet who doesn't remember the language her grand-father taught her?

What good is a poet who sees the power of those words manifested on us and in us?

They stole our speech and raped our minds.

If love could be made visible, would it be in the enemy's language? It is the only weapon I hold: this pen, this knife, this tool, this language.

The writer has to tell. It is the weapon I know how to use.

*Dear Diary*, did you give her what she needs? Did you back away in horror at the pain of her life? Did you open beneath her to receive the blows of her testimony? Did you wrap your pages around her incest-battered body? Did you make her feel clean again, innocent?

Yellow paper, please give me what I need.

Pen, be my strength.

If love could be made visible, would it be on the skins of trees, this paper spread out beneath my hands?

*Who will heal the healer?*\* Dennis Maracle

Love as piercing as the screwdriver's thrust.

Love as searing as the marks on an infant's leg.

Love as clear as her face.

Love as clean as a sheet of yellow paper.

Love as honest as a poem.

I have to tell.

It is the only thing I know to do.

November 1989
Toronto, Canada

\*Conversation with the author.

# This Is History

*for Donna Goodleaf*

Long before there was an earth and long before there were people called human, there was a Sky World.

On Sky World there were Sky People who were like us and not like us. And of the Sky People there was Sky Woman. Sky Woman had a peculiar trait: she had curiosity. She bothered the others with her questions, with wanting to know what lay beneath the clouds that supported her world. Sometimes she pushed the clouds aside and looked down through her world to the large expanse of blue that shimmered below. The others were tired of her peculiar trait and called her an aberration, a queer woman who asked questions, a woman who wasn't satisfied with what she had.

Sky Woman spent much of her time dreaming—dreaming about the blue expanse underneath the clouds, dreaming about floating through the clouds, dreaming about the blue color and how it would feel to her touch. One day she pushed the clouds away from her and leaned out of the opening. She fell. The others tried to catch her hands and pull her back, but she struggled free and began to float downward. The Sky People watched her descent and agreed that they were glad to see her go. She was a nuisance with her questions, an aberration, a queer woman who was not like them—content to walk the clouds undisturbed.

Sky Woman floated. The currents of wind played through her hair. She put out her arms and felt the sensations of air between her fingers. She kicked her legs, did somersaults, and was curious about the free, delightful feelings of flying. Faster, faster, she floated toward the blue shimmer that beckoned her.

She heard a noise and turned to see a beautiful creature with black wings and a white head flying close to her. The creature spoke. "I am Eagle. I have been sent to carry you to your new home." Sky Woman laughed and held out her hands for Eagle to brush his wings against. He swooped under her, and she settled on his back. They flew. They circled, they glided, they flew, Sky Woman clutching the feathers of the great creature.

Sky Woman looked down at the blue color. Rising from the expanse was a turtle. Turtle looked up at the flying pair and nodded her head. She dove into the waters and came up again with a muskrat clinging to her back. In Muskrat's paw was a clump of dark brown dirt scooped from the bottom of the sea. She laid it on Turtle's back and jumped back into the water. Sky Woman watched the creature swim away, her long tail skimming the top of the waves, her whiskers shining. Sky Woman watched as the dark brown dirt began to spread. All across Turtle's back the dirt was spreading, spreading, and in this dirt green things were growing. Small green things, tall green things, and in the middle of Turtle's back, the tallest thing grew. It grew branches and needles, more and more branches, until it reached where Eagle and Sky Woman were hovering.

Turtle raised her head and beckoned to the pair. Eagle flew down to Turtle's back and gently lay Sky Woman on the soft dirt. Then he flew to the very top of the White Pine tree and said, "I will be here, watching over everything that is to be. You will look to me as the harbinger of what is to happen. You will be kind to me and my people. In return, I will keep this place safe." Eagle folded his wings and looked away.

Sky Woman felt the soft dirt with her fingers. She brought the dirt to her mouth and tasted the color of it. She looked around at the green things. Some were flowering with fantastic shapes. She stood on her feet and felt the solid back of Turtle beneath her. She marveled at this wonderful place and wondered what she would do here.

Turtle swiveled her head and looked at Sky Woman with ancient eyes. "You will live here and make this a new place. You will be kind, and you will call me Mother. I will make all manner of creatures and growing things to guide you on this new place. You will watch them carefully, and from them you will learn how to live. You will take care to be respectful and honorable to me. I am your Mother." Sky Woman touched Turtle's back and promised to honor and respect her. She lay down on Turtle's back and fell asleep.

As she slept, Turtle grew. Her back became wider and longer. She slapped her tail and cracks appeared in her back. From these cracks came mountains, canyons were formed, rivers and lakes were made from the spit of Turtle's mouth. She shook her body and prairies sprang up, deserts settled, marshes and wetlands pushed their way through the cracks of Turtle's shell. Turtle opened her mouth and called. Creatures came crawling out of her back. Some had wings, some had four legs, six legs, or eight. Some had no legs but slithered on the ground, some had no legs and swam with fins. These creatures crawled out of Turtle's back and some were covered with fur, some with feathers, some with scales, some with skins of beautiful colors. Turtle called again, and the creatures found their voice. Some sang, some barked, some growled and roared, some had no voice but a hiss, some had no voice and rubbed their legs together to speak. Turtle called again. The creatures began to make homes. Some gathered twigs and leaves, others spun webs, some found caves, others dug holes in the ground. Some made the waters their home, and some of these came up for air to breathe. Turtle shuddered, and the new place was made a continent, a world.

Turtle gave a last look to the sleeping Sky Woman. "Inside you is growing a being who is like you and not like you. This being will be your companion. Together you will give names to the creatures and growing things. You will be kind to these things. This companion growing inside you will be called First Woman, for she will be the first of these beings on this earth. Together you will respect me and call me Mother. Listen to the voices of the creatures and communicate with them. This will be called prayer, for prayer is the language of all my creations. Remember me." Turtle rested from her long labor.

Sky Woman woke and touched herself. Inside her body she felt the stirrings of another. She stood on her feet and walked the earth. She climbed mountains, she walked in the desert, she slept in trees, she listened to the voices of the creatures and living things, she swam in the waters, she smelled the growing things that came from the earth. As she wandered and discovered, her body grew from the being inside her. She ate leaves, she picked fruit. An animal showed her how to bring fire, then threw himself in the flames that she might eat of him. She prayed her thanks, remembering Turtle's words. Sky Woman watched the creatures, learning how they lived in community with each other, learning how they hunted, how they stored food, how they prayed. Her body grew larger, and she felt her companion move inside her, waiting to be born. She watched the living things, seeing how they fed their young, how they taught their young, how they protected their young. She watched and learned and saw how things should be. She waited for the day when First Woman would come and together they would be companions, lovers of the earth, namers of all things, planters and harvesters, creators.

On a day when Sky Woman was listening to the animals, she felt a sharp pain inside of her. First Woman wanted to be born. Sky Woman walked the earth, looking for soft things to lay her companion on when she was born. She gathered all day, finding feathers of the winged-creatures, skins of the fur-bearers. She gathered these things and made a deep nest. She gathered other special things for medicine and magic. She ate leaves from a plant that eased her pain. She clutched her magic things in her hands to give her help. She prayed to the creatures to strengthen her. She squatted over the deep nest and began to push. She pushed and held tight to the magic medicine. She pushed, and First Woman slipped out of her and onto the soft nest. First Woman gave a cry. Sky Woman touched her companion, then gave another great push as her placenta fell from her. She cut the long cord with her teeth as she had learned from the animals. She ate the placenta as she had learned from the animals. She brought First Woman to her breast as she had learned, and First Woman began to suckle, drawing nourishment and medicine from Sky Woman.

Sky Woman prayed, thanking the creatures for teaching her how to give birth. She touched the earth, thanking Mother for giving her this gift of a companion. Turtle shuddered, acknowledging the prayer. That day, Sky Woman began a new thing. She opened her mouth and sounds came forth. Sounds of song. She sang and began a new thing—singing prayers. She fashioned a thing out of animal skin and wood. She touched the thing and it resonated. She touched it again and called it drum. She sang with the rhythm of her touching. First Woman suckled as her companion sang the prayers.

First Woman began to grow. In the beginning she lay in her nest dreaming, then crying out as she wanted to suckle. Then she opened her eyes and saw her companion and smiled. Then she sat up and made sounds. Then she crawled and was curious about everything. She wanted to touch and feel and taste all that was around her. Sky Woman carried her on her back when she walked the earth, listening to the living things and talking with them. First Woman saw all the things that Sky Woman pointed out to her. She listened to Sky Woman touch the drum and make singing prayers. First Woman stood on her feet and felt the solid shell of Turtle against her feet. The two companions began walking together. First Woman made a drum for herself, and together the companions made magic by touching their drums and singing their prayers. First Woman grew, and as she grew Sky Woman showed her the green things, the animal things, the living things, and told her they needed to name them. Together they began the naming. Heron, bear, snake, dolphin, spider, maple, oak, thistle, cricket, wolf, hawk, trout, goldenrod, firefly. They named together and in naming, the women became closer and truer companions. The living things that now had names moved closer to the women and taught them how to dance. Together, they all danced as the women touched their drums and made their singing prayers. Together they danced. Together. All together.

In time the women observed the changes that took place around them. They observed that sometimes the trees would shed their leaves and at other times would grow new ones. They observed that some creatures buried themselves in caves and burrows and slept for long times, reappearing when the trees began their new birth. They observed that some creatures flew away for long times, reappearing when the animals crawled from their caves and dens. Together, the companions decided they would sing special songs and different prayers when the earth was changing and the creatures were changing. They named these times seasons and made different drums, sewn with feathers and stones. The companions wore stones around their necks, feathers in their hair, and shells on their feet, and when they danced, the music was new and extraordinary. They prepared feasts at this time, asking the animals to accept their death. Some walked into their arrows, some ran away. The animals that gave their lives were thanked and their bones were buried in Turtle's back to feed her—the Mother of all things.

The women fashioned combs from animal teeth and claws. They spent long times combing and caressing each other's hair. They crushed berries and flowers and painted signs on their bodies to honor Mother and the living things who lived with them. They painted on rocks and stones to honor the creatures who taught them. They fixed food together, feeding each other herbs and roots and plants. They lit fires together and cooked the foods that gave them strength and medicine. They laughed together and made language between them. They touched each other and in the touching made a new word: love. They touched each other and made a language of touching: passion. They made medicine together. They made magic together.

And on a day when First Woman woke from her sleep, she bled from her body. Sky Woman marveled at this thing her companion could do because she was born on Turtle's back. Sky Woman built a special place for her companion to retreat at this time, for it was wondrous what her body could do. First Woman went to her bleeding-place and dreamed about her body and the magic it made. And at the end of this time, she emerged laughing and holding out her arms to Sky Woman.

Time went by, long times went by. Sky Woman felt her body changing. Her skin was wrinkling, her hands were not as strong. She could not hunt as she used to. Her eyes were becoming dim, her sight unclear. She walked the earth in this changed body and took longer to climb mountains and swim in the waters. She still enjoyed the touch of First Woman, the laughter and language they shared between them, the dancing, the singing prayers. But her body was changed. Sky Woman whispered to Mother, asking her what these changes meant. Mother whispered back that Sky Woman was aged and soon her body would stop living. Before this event happened, Sky Woman must give her companion instruction. Mother and Sky Woman whispered together as First Woman slept. They whispered together the long night through.

When First Woman woke from her sleep, Sky Woman told her of the event that was to happen. "You must cut the heart from this body and bury it in the field by your bleeding-place. Then you must cut this body in small pieces and fling them into the sky. You will do this for me."

And the day came that Sky Woman's body stopped living. First Woman touched her companion's face and promised to carry out her request. She carved the heart from Sky Woman's body and buried it in the open field near her bleeding-place. She put her ear to the ground and heard Sky Woman's voice, "From this place will grow three plants. As long as they grow, you will never want for food or magic. Name these plants corn, beans, and squash. Call them the Three Sisters, for like us, they will never grow apart."

First Woman watched as the green plant burst from the ground, growing stalks that bore ears of beautifully colored kernels. From beneath the corn rose another plant with small leaves, and it twined around the stalks carrying pods of green. Inside each pod were small, white beans. From under the beans came a sprawling vine with large leaves that tumbled and grew and shaded the beans' delicate roots. On this vine were large, green squash that grew and turned orange and yellow. Three Sisters, First Woman named them.

First Woman cut her companion's body in small pieces and flung them at the sky. The sky turned dark, and there, glittering and shining, were bright-colored stars and a round moon. The moon spoke. "I will come to you every day when the sun is sleeping. You will make songs and prayers for me. Inside you are growing two beings. They are not like us. They are called Twin Sons. One of these is good and will honor us and our Mother. One of these is not good and will bring things that we have no names for. Teach these beings what we have learned together. Teach them that if the sons do not honor the women who made them, that will be the end of this earth. Keep well, my beloved First Woman. Eagle is watching out for you. Honor the living things. Be kind to them. Be strong. I am always with you. Remember our Mother. Be kind to her."

First Woman touched her body, feeling the movements inside. She touched the back of Mother and waited for the beings who would change her world.

# Wild Turkeys

Violet smiled when she saw the sign: Welcome to Fairview, Wild Turkey Capital of Michigan. The sign had been there for as long as she could remember, the same tired old bird peering out from behind the letters. Over the years the vivid colors of the bird's feathers had dulled to a light brown, and the black lettering was now a washed-out grey. Violet had lived nearby before she ran away. But she remembered the sign and remembered the wild turkeys.

She was six or seven when she'd seen them. While playing in the field near her home, she came across them pecking for food and moving silently on the ground. She thought they were ugly birds until they spread their wings and skittered away from her. Then the rich reds, rusts, and browns were displayed for her to see. They flew low over the field, not reaching any great height, almost as if it were a struggle to get off the ground. She had run home to tell her mom about the birds. Her mom told Violet a story.

"In the old days, sweetie, the turkey used to fly real high. Almost as high as a hawk. There was an animal, a porcupine, who got jealous of the turkey's pretty colors and the way she could fly. See, the porcupine was kinda ugly. One night when the turkey was sleeping, the porcupine sneaked up and clipped her wings with his sharp claws. After that, the turkey couldn't fly very far or very high, but she still kept her pretty feathers. The porcupine made the Creator so mad, he gave him those long, sharp quills so nobody would go near him anymore."

"That's sad, Mom."

"Well, lots of things are sad, Violet. But the turkey kept her feathers and she's still alive. I think that's the important thing."

Slowing down the car to get a good look at the sign, she saw another across the street: Rita's Diner. She didn't remember the diner; it must be new. She was hungry and needed some coffee to fortify her for the two hours of driving she still had ahead of her. She pulled into the lot and sat for a few minutes, checking her money supply and cleaning her glasses. She had spent more than she'd planned on this trip back to see her grandmother. She had bought a birdhouse for Grandma who loved to sit and watch the birds that came to visit her yard. The birdhouse was a fancy one, handmade, with dozens of small holes for the birds to nest. Violet had set it up by the front window where Grandma spent most of her day, looking out at the trees and rose bushes.

"Can't you stay longer, Violet? It's been so long since I seen you. Talking on the phone's not the same as having my best girl here."

Violet had looked at her grandmother's old, lined face, the brown eyes full of life and curiosity. "I'm starting my new job tomorrow, but I promise I'll come back more often, Grandma. I'll be making more money so I can afford the travel as long as the car holds out. If it weren't for you and the money you've given me, I don't know what I would have done. But I'll be back. I'm not scared anymore."

"You shouldn't be. He's long gone, can't hurt you no more. And the money," Grandma waved away the hundreds of dollars she had sent to Violet, "what have I got to spend it on?"

"You don't have that much, Grandma."

"I don't need much. Now that I got this fancy birdhouse, I got everything I need," and she had pulled Violet to her and kissed her.

Violet entered the diner, noting the smallness and cleanliness of the place. There were only a few tables, no booths, and the walls were painted a sun yellow. Red-and-white checked curtains hung at the scrubbed windows. She sat down at a table and looked around the space, grinning when she saw the stuffed turkey mounted on a wall. Turkeys were evident most everywhere. Turkey salt-and-pepper shakers were sitting on each table. Her napkin, aligned in front of her, had knife, fork, and spoon lying on top of a foolishly smiling turkey. There were photographs and paintings of wild turkeys hanging on the walls.

A waitress with improbable red-lacquered hair came over and poured coffee into the thick white mug resting beside the smiling turkey. Violet noticed the woman's hands were chapped and red. She looked up and smiled her thanks. The pin on the woman's yellow uniform said Rita. Violet looked around the room as she sipped her coffee. A group of men were sitting at a table by the window. Across from her, a woman was eating from a plate of french fries, her black hair pulled back into a ponytail, secured with two beaded barrettes. The woman smiled shyly at Violet and resumed eating her fries.

"You hear about Rosie?" the waitress inquired to no one in particular. "After all these years she finally left that bastard."

Violet tensed in her chair and drank her coffee.

The men acknowledged they'd heard the news. "Wonder where she went?" one of them asked, an expression of boredom on his face. The other men shrugged.

Rita said, "I don't know, but I tell you, I wouldn't say even if I did know. That Billy's a mean son-of-a-bitch. He'd go after her and probably kill her this time."

Violet felt a wave of fear flush through her body. She sat like a rock, afraid to move.

Rita continued. "That Billy come in here looking for Rosie. Said she stole his money and took off. Butter wouldn't melt in his mouth when he was talking to me. Like I don't know what kinda man he is. Son-of-a-bitch. As if he ever made a dime on his own, the lazy bum, living off of Rosie and her wages here."

Her mouth bleeding, Violet tried to reach the door. He pulled her back and smacked her face again. Hot tears stung her eyes and she couldn't see where the next blow was coming from, but she felt it, landing on her nose. A new flow of blood to add to the rest. "Lazy bitch. Can't even have my dinner ready when I get home. You know I like my dinner on time." The blows were coming from all directions now. How could one man have so many hands? The thought snapped across her mind as she struggled to get free. Don't fight him, he'll just get meaner. She tasted the blood in her mouth and bent over to retrieve her glasses. Broken. Again. A last kick to her butt. "I'll get your dinner."

Violet's hand trembled as she picked up her mug and drank the cooling liquid. Rita came over and poured more coffee. "You want anything to eat, honey? Our special is meat loaf sandwich, lots of gravy. I make the pies myself, so I know they're good." Rita's face was heavily made up: beige foundation, rose-colored rouge, blue eye shadow, black mascara, and red lipstick. Her face was kind and tired.

Violet wanted to leave but felt like she was welded to her chair. "I guess a piece of pie would be nice."

"Apple, cherry, pumpkin, strawberry, blueberry, or chocolate?"

"Cherry, please." Why did she always sound so meek? She cleared her throat. "I changed my mind. Apple."

"You're entitled," Rita said, as she went to get the pie. Bringing the slab of sugared crust leaking with fat slices of apples and cinnamon, Rita continued her tirade against Billy. "That man! Thought I never noticed Rosie's black eyes, her bruises. And that broken arm. Fell down the stairs, my foot! He probably pushed her. Twenty years married to that bum. Thank god, they didn't have any kids. I told her, I said, 'Rosie, you can't let him do that to you.' Said it so many times she must have got sick hearing me. More coffee, Cheryl?" Rita held up the pot and looked toward the woman eating the french fries.

"Yes, I could do with another cup." Cheryl's voice was soft. She glanced at Violet and smiled again. "You from around here?"

"I used to live near here. I'm just up visiting my grandma. I'm on my way home right now." Violet wanted to leave. She lurched from her chair and it made a loud scraping sound on the floor. The men turned to look at her. She fled to the washroom.

Broken arm. "I think my arm's broken. Please, I think you broke my arm." A kick to her stomach. "That right? Maybe I'll break the other one, bitch. You know I like starch in my shirts. Can't you do anything right?" The fist on her back, pounding on her back. Blows on her head. The arm dangling at her side, her useful one raised to stop the fists. Burning pain in her arm. She couldn't breathe from the pain. The fists pounding on her back, her shoulders. It stopped. "Get me a beer. Better go get that arm fixed. Dumb bitch." She'd get her arm fixed. Fell down the stairs. Again. How many times can you fall down the stairs before someone notices how accident-prone you are? Dumb bitch. She'd better think of a new excuse from now on.

Violet looked in the mirror of the washroom and rubbed her arm. He always called her dumb and ugly. She stared intently at the image in the mirror. Her new haircut took her by surprise. The short hair where there used to be a long, brown tangle. She adjusted the glasses on her nose. She wasn't ugly. Dumb maybe, for staying with him so long. She smiled at her reflection. I got away, didn't I?

She came out of the washroom and noticed that the men had left. She sat down to eat her pie. Cheryl was watching Rita clear the table where the men had been.

Rita stacked the dishes and carried them into the kitchen. She came out immediately. "I'll get to those later. Those old farts," she jerked her head to indicate the empty table. "They could care less about Rosie. Probably side with Billy. I tell you, men are all alike. Think a wife's there to get screwed and clean up their messes." She shook her head, the stiff red helmet of hair not moving an inch. "You married, hon?" she inquired of Violet.

"No."

"Smart girl. You get married and they just think they can boss you around to suit them. I guess you, me, and Cheryl's the only smart women left in this town. A couple of bachelorettes, that's us." Rita snorted and went back to the kitchen.

Violet finished her pie. She had wanted cherry, but the apple was good and filled the hollow space inside. From the kitchen came the sounds of dishes clattering and water being run. "Damn that Billy! Lost a waitress and I have to put up with him, sneaking around here and asking questions."

Cheryl said, "Rita's mad. Not about losing a waitress but about losing a friend. Rosie was a good woman."

"You act like she's dead," Violet said angrily. "More power to her, I say."

Cheryl looked surprised. "I know. I think the same as you. It takes guts to do what she did."

Guts. "I hate your guts, bitch." The slap in the face, the punch in the stomach. Her glasses flying off her face. "I don't know why you can't do anything right. Jesus Christ, this place is a pigsty. But that figures, a pig like you. Squaw. Can't even keep a man's house clean." She hurried to pick the newspapers off the floor and stacked them neatly on the table. "Come here." "No." "Come here!" Of course she went. His hands on her body, his mouth forcing hers open, his tongue pushing down her throat. "Bitch." As he raped her on the floor, her eyes wandered to the neat stack of newspapers sitting on the table. She looked at the table while he pushed and shoved inside her, her arms outflung at her sides. Finished. She lay on the floor, not sure of what he expected of her now. "Get me a beer."

"You O.K.?" Cheryl asked, concern on her face.

"Yeah. I was thinking of . . . nothing."

Rita came bustling out of the kitchen, carrying pies that she carefully set in the plastic covered containers by the coffee pot. Getting a rag, she began washing down the tables, checking the ketchup and mustard bottles, realigning the salt-and-pepper shakers. "Can I get you girls anything?"

Cheryl held up her mug to indicate more coffee.

Rita poured. "I tell you, I was just in the kitchen thinking about Rosie, wondering where she was. Do you think she went to one of them shelters? But how could she get there? And why didn't she call me? I would have driven her anywhere. Billy never let her drive his car, and she didn't have one. *His* car. As if her money didn't pay for it. God, I hate that man! Never could stand the sight of him. Strutting in here like some prize package. I never knew what she saw in him in the first place. Me and Rosie go way back together. Do you think she'll call me when she gets settled? You don't think she'll come back, do you? I'd sooner never see her again than think she might go back to that bastard." Rita's face was worried.

"No, I don't think she'll come back," Cheryl answered.

"Well, how do you know she won't? I remember one time she ran away and was staying with me. We had the best time together, then he comes crawling up to the door, begging her to come home. 'I didn't mean it,' he says, in that spineless voice of his. She looked at me like to say, what can I do? I know what she could have done. Stayed with me.

"Billy was afraid of me. Oh, he hated me, it was plain on his face, but he was scared of me just the same. She went back and he musta beat her real bad that time 'cause she called in to say she got the flu and wouldn't be in to work for a few days. I says to her, Rose Helen, I'm coming right over there to get you. But no, she wouldn't hear of it. I just got the flu, she says. So I let her be."

Rita wrung the cloth in her hands, the strong tendons standing out like ropes. "I'm glad she got away. Too bad she didn't shoot him and burn the house down, like that woman a few years back. Oh, Rosie." Her eyes became bright and wet, and she turned away and went into the kitchen.

She ran away, but she didn't have anywhere to go. She thought of calling Grandma, but Grandma didn't know the

things he did to her and he might hurt Grandma if she took
Violet in. She called in sick to work and took a bus to Traverse City. She wandered the streets, looking in shop windows, looking into people's faces. Nobody knew her here.
Nobody knew what he did when the door was closed. Nobody knew. She pretended she was someone else. Just a
woman going shopping, leisurely, taking her time, enjoy-
ing a day out. The freedom. The freedom of walking up the
street. She was another person, not the dumb, ugly squaw
he said she was. Even her body felt different. Like it be-
longed to her. *Her.* What would happen if she stayed here?
She couldn't. She didn't have any money, only the clothes
she was wearing, no place to stay. What was she thinking
of? Not possible, not possible. She took the bus home. Of
course he knew she had run away. She should have known
he would find out. He cried this time. Promised he wouldn't
hurt her anymore. Said he was scared she had left him for
good. Promised he wouldn't hurt her anymore. She believed
him. What else could she do, a dumb, ugly bitch like herself? Later that night he stomped on her feet and legs as
if to punish the very limbs that dared to go walking, like
a *real* person, up the street in Traverse City.

Violet looked up from the table. Cheryl was watching her, a look
of sympathy in her lively brown eyes. "So you were visiting your
grandma? Do you have other family here?"

"No. My mother died when I was twelve. My dad . . . I don't know
where my dad is. I went to live with my grandma after Mom died.
I haven't been back here for a while, about a year. My grandma's getting old, and I like to check on her, you know, see for myself how
she's doing. I'd like her to come and live with me. She says she'll see,
but I think that means no. She wouldn't like the city unless I could
find a place that had a little grass or some trees. But I'm looking
for a new place. Right now, I'm living in kind of a dump." Violet
stopped. She could feel her cheeks getting hot. She never talked

this much. "Are you from around here?" she asked Cheryl, anxious to get the conversation away from herself.

"No, I'm from Peshawbestown, the reservation past Traverse City. I'm just here for the summer, working in a place for women and children. We're starting something similar in my community, and I'm here to learn the ropes." Cheryl's full lips curved into a smile. "Naturally, our place will be more 'Indian style.' "

"My mother was from there."

"No kidding! What was her name? Maybe I know your family," Cheryl asked eagerly.

"I don't know her maiden name." What a stupid thing to say, Violet thought. What possible harm could come from telling Cheryl her mother's name? Was she going to live like this forever, afraid to tell people anything?

Rita hurried out of the kitchen. "Thought I heard the door. Must be going crazy! For a minute there, I thought it was Rosie. Didn't know whether to be mad or glad. You get my age, you start imagining things." She smiled weakly.

Cheryl said, "Your age indeed. You don't look a day over thirty-five."

Rita touched her hair. "Well, the dye job helps, don't it? Thirty-five, my foot! Thought I was the snow-job queen around here."

Cheryl and Rita laughed. Even Violet joined in, though her laugh was rusty and unused.

"I'll get you girls more coffee, then I think I'll join you and have a cigarette. Trying to quit," she said ruefully to Violet, "but it's only my second one today."

She brought the pot over and gestured to Violet. "Come on over here and sit with us."

Violet pulled out a chair and sat stiffly holding her coffee cup, pretending this was the most natural thing in the world for her to do—sit with women, share stories, share life.

"Well, this is nice," Rita took a deep drag from her cigarette and blew the smoke out gustily. "Just us girls. I can't get my mind off Rosie. Two days she's been gone and not a word. Not that I expect her to be rushing to a phone to call me. I expect this is the first time in her life she's had some breathing space. But I do want to hear from her.

"Ever since we was kids I've been worrying about her. Her dad was the biggest drunk in town. I know he used to beat Rosie's ma. I heard my own folks talking when they thought I wasn't listening. Rosie used to tell me things too. I won't repeat them. The woman's gotta have some dignity. It just got to be a natural thing. I'd think up ways to get Rosie out of that house, away from her dad. She slept over our house so much, my ma said she might as well adopt her. Oh, I prayed for that to happen, I did. We were like twins, never apart.

"And when we were teens, didn't that big, ugly Billy Claymore come into our lives and spoil everything. What she saw in him I just don't. . .well, I guess he was good to her for a while, made her think he'd take care of her. I saw right through him, but she wouldn't listen to me."

Rita puffed angrily at her cigarette and tapped the ashes into a metal tray. "She wouldn't listen to me. I was maid of honor at her wedding. Not much of a wedding, just standing in front of the justice of the peace. I helped her pick out her dress. It was pink and had a full skirt. We starched her crinolines so the dress stuck out real far. She looked so pretty. And happy. I'll guarantee that was the last happy day she had with that man. First and last!" She stubbed out her cigarette and lit a fresh one. "I cried. Told her I always cry at weddings. She would have believed anything on that day.

"She had on this cute little hat. White, with a veil that came down to her nose. She gave me that hat some years back. Said it just took up space in her closet. It looked like hell on me, but I kept it anyways. Girls, it's a terrible thing when you can't help a friend." She stubbed out her second cigarette with force.

"It sounds to me," Cheryl said, taking Rita's hand, "like you helped her all you could. You were a good friend to her. Most women don't have that."

"That's right," Violet blurted. "Women like that. . .we. . .they don't have any friends. Too scared or ashamed. . .or something."

Her voice trailed away.

Rita squinted her eyes and gave Violet a long look. "You think she'll be O.K.?"

> Her mother didn't have friends. "Just you and me, Violet. You're the best friend a mother ever needs." But she couldn't be the kind of friend her mom needed, the kind that would protect her from the jealous rampages of a husband. She was a little girl, not a grownup who could stand up to her father. And after her mom died from the cancer, he came to her and wanted to touch her, wanted to do things to her. What had she done to make him want to do things that only grownups are supposed to do? Was it because her body had matured so fast? She had started her period when she was eleven and her breasts got bigger and she started to grow hair under her arms and on her private place. *Private place.* That's what her mom used to call it. Was that why her dad wanted her to do things that she wasn't supposed to do? And then Grandma, her precious grandma, had come to take her to live with her. "You're not fit to raise this child," Grandma had told her father. "You're not fit." She had never told Grandma about the grown-up things dad had wanted her to do. Did she know? But if she'd known, would she have wanted Violet anyway? Violet never told, fearing the answer to the question she carried in her twelve-year-old heart. And it settled in her heart that it must have been her fault—her mother's beatings, her father's seductions—and she vowed to be a good girl from now on. Try to please everyone. Try very hard to please.

Cheryl was talking. "I bet she went to a shelter. They'll take good care of her there. She'll call you when she's got herself together, I'm sure of it."

"A while back I saw this TV show," Rita lit up another cigarette. "There was a woman on there from the shelter. She talked about women hating themselves and thinking they deserved the beatings they was getting. I thought, that's my Rose Helen. No matter how many times I told her she was worth something, that she was a wonderful woman, *she* didn't believe it, so why would she believe me? At the end of the show they gave some numbers to call. I copied them down and gave them to Rosie. What's this? she said. I told her they was phone numbers for women shelters. A woman could go there and get away from her husband and they'd keep her safe. She gave me a look, I tell you, I don't ever want to see that look again. Like a whipped dog. Like she was ashamed 'cause her own husband was beating on her. Like it was all her fault! I tell you, girls, I like to die to see that look on my Rose Helen's face." Rita's mascara was running in dark rivers down her face, and she lifted a hand to wipe away the black smudges. Violet handed her a napkin, the smiling turkeys a malicious joke against Rita's pain-filled face as she wiped her eyes. "I'm not a praying woman, but I pray that Rosie's safe and learning how to love herself. Like I love her."

*Love yourself.* Her counselor had brought that incredible, unthinkable idea to Violet. It took her days to sort through the thoughts that were making a mess in her brain. Wasn't it enough that she had found strength to leave her husband? Finally making that call to the shelter, to her grandma, who had saved her once and now had to do it again. Must she think about loving herself? A dumb, ugly bitch? A squaw? A pig? A woman who couldn't make dinner on time, starch his shirts right, pick up newspapers that she dared to read and leave lying on the floor? Her self? Love? Slowly, so slowly, she started to put the little scraps together, the bits of herself that she could love. Like piecing together a quilt, she basted the parts in her mind with fragile thread. It wasn't finished yet, but someday the cloth would be whole and she would cover herself with the multicolored blocks.

"My mother's name was Johnson." Violet looked at Cheryl and

smiled.

"I know so many Johnsons, it'll take us forever to figure it out," Cheryl laughed, touching Violet's hand delicately with her own.

Violet reached for her coffee and relaxed in her chair. Cheryl gave her hand a last pat and asked, "You ever gone back to where your mom came from?"

"No, but I've thought about it. You know, just to see where she lived when she was a girl. She used to talk about it, and so did my grandma. They moved from there when my mom was just a kid. Maybe the next time I come here, I'll drive up that way and take Grandma too."

"You do that, honey," Rita piped in. "And when you do, be sure to stop by here and see me." She blew her nose and got up, gathering the ashtray and coffee mug. "Just help yourself to more coffee, girls. I'll be in the kitchen doing up the dishes. Maybe I'll put together more pies. Supper crowd's gonna be coming in soon." She made her way to the kitchen, turning to smile at Cheryl and Violet. "You girls sure were a blessing to me today. I just know Rosie's gonna be O.K. I *feel* it somehow. And I'll be there for her, like I always been." Rita smiled again, her face transformed into that of a young woman. She went through the kitchen door, her red hair blazing like a flag.

"I guess I better get going," Violet said. "I'm starting a new job tomorrow and there's a million things I need to do, plus two more hours of driving ahead of me."

"Good luck with your new job. You know, Rosie's O.K. She's at the shelter where I work. I can't tell Rita, but I think I wanted to come in here today just to reassure her." Cheryl looked sad. "I didn't know Rita loved her so much."

"I'm glad I met you, Cheryl. Maybe we'll see each other again."

"Well, just to make sure, here's my name and address. I'll be home in October. You bring your grandma, and we'll track down those people of yours." She dug in her purse and wrote down the information on a slip of paper. "I hope you come. Everyone should know where they're from, where home is." She handed Violet the paper, their hands touching briefly.

Violet got out her wallet and left a five-dollar bill on the table. "I'll be back. Thank you, Cheryl."

"For what?"

"Oh, caring about Rita and Rosie. Everything." Violet slung her purse over her shoulder. "Tell Rita good-bye for me. Tell her. . .tell her that it might take a long time, but Rosie will make it." She smiled into Cheryl's face.

She walked out of the diner and got in her car. Turning on the ignition, Violet looked once again at the sign of the wild turkey.

"Sometimes we fly real high."

# Home Coming

She felt the thud before it registered in her mind that she had struck something in the road.

She braked the car, turned off the motor, and sat. It couldn't have been a dog or a child, though god knows, she thought angrily, there are too many of those species on this goddamn island. The woman's mouth formed into a straight, bitter line. She pushed her dark, long hair over her shoulders and sat, staring out the front windshield at the full moon that seemed to be careening down on top of her. The Harvest Moon, the whites called it. She had forgotten the Indian words for this kind of moon. There was a lot to harvest around here, she thought: kids, dogs, booze, the occasional gunshot heard on a Friday or Saturday night; the plentiful yelling, screaming, and fighting that came before the occasional gunshot.

The Harvest Moon.

Granny died today.

The woman unbuckled her seat belt, irritated that she was so careful of herself inside a car when she was so careless inside her life. She opened the car door, listening for a sound that might identify what it was she had hit. There were no whimpering noises like a child or dog would make. Or the screaming that rabbits make when they are dying.

The woman had a surge of memory of the first time Grampa had taken her out to shoot rabbits.

"You have to be fast," Grampa said. "Rabbits freeze for a few seconds, but then they move real quick, so you only got that second to take good aim."

He demonstrated his technique four times—each time a true shot, each time an instantly dead rabbit. The girl carried the canvas sack filling with rabbits, the sack warm against her side. Grampa had wanted five rabbits that day. He had decided that was his quota. Grampa's quotas were never the same, and the woman never found out how he came to his decisions. He had died before she remembered to ask.

The fifth rabbit jumped in front of them. Taking aim, Grampa shot. The rabbit fell into a cover of weeds, and the screaming began. The girl looked at her grampa, hot tears beginning to course down her cheeks. Grampa ran to the weeds, pulled out the rabbit, and wrung its neck. The rabbit was silenced.

"This is a bad thing, Granddaughter. I did not kill this rabbit proper. No animal should scream like that. I must be getting old if I make an animal scream like that."

Grampa had buried the rabbit, rather than putting it in the sack. He said it wouldn't be right to leave it for the crows; it had not died proper. He took her hand saying, "I am tired, Granddaughter. Take me home."

It occurred to the woman standing outside the car that Grampa had indeed become old that day. His face, a mass of lines and cracks, seemed to sag into itself. He smiled at the girl holding his hand, but the smile was more a grimace than the sweet curve of mouth that was his usual expression. "I'm gettin' old, eh?"

She hadn't remembered to ask him about his system of rabbit quotas. Now it seemed important that she should have.

The woman heard a rustling on the right side of the car. As she cautiously walked around the car, the rustling became louder. Then she saw it. A blue heron. It was struggling to rise, to attempt a flight that even the woman, who did not fly, knew was impossible. She felt a scream pushing through her body. "My first time back on this goddamn island in five years and I do this! I hate this place. Even the herons are cursed. They walk in front of cars and get killed. I hate this place! I didn't want to come back here. I didn't. I didn't."

This is a bad thing, Granddaughter.

The woman wept, her hands drawn into fists that she raised to the moon, as if to smash the golden light into splinters. But the moon's brightness remained steady, its face relentless on her power-less fists. Hundreds of tiny moons made a path down the woman's cheeks as the light reflected off each tear that came from her grey eyes. She walked toward the heron. It attempted to rise, the long neck trying to unfold, the beak moving back and forth, back and forth with a jerky rhythm. The bird made no sound. The woman reached out, her fingers wanting to touch the heron. She touched it. The heron's neck sprang forward, then receded. The bird became still, its opaque eyes on the woman. She put her arms about the bird and sat on the road. She could feel a heartbeat under her fingers.

Granny. Oh, Granny. When Brother called me today, I knew what he was going to say. I tried to keep him from saying it. "She's dead, Sister. Our granny is dead. Please come to help me get her ready. She wants you to come and help me get her ready. Her last words were about you." His quiet voice went on in the familiar ca-dence. "I have missed you too. I have prayed that you would come back to us. At night, I would look over the river and try to see you and I would call to you. Did you ever hear me, Sister?"

The woman wanted to scream into the phone, yes, I heard your voice, constantly at me, constantly in my dreams, always at me to come home to that island. Instead she replied, "No, Brother, I didn't hear you. You know I left it all behind." She could hear her brother sigh. "Will you come back this one time? To help with our granny?" She made her own sigh. "Yes, I'll be there as soon as I can." Her older brother began to sob and the woman was stunned, then an-gry, that her brother could cry over the wires while she stood help-less in her apartment, holding on for dear life to the telephone, not shedding a tear.

I'm holding a dying bird. I'm sitting in the road like some crazy woman, talking to myself. But that's who I talk to—myself. Granny, you told me I was special, I was *Nishnawbe*, I was different from Mum.

You said I wouldn't make the same mistakes she made. Oh, I made them, Granny. I made them. I hated you and Grampa making excuses for her. The time I ran after her, begging her to come back in the house. "You care more about your friends than you do about us," I yelled at her. Mum kept on walking, looking for the booze, the party, the men. She didn't even look back at me. Granny, you and Grampa and Brother came to take my hands to pull me away from the night, from the picture of Mum walking down the road, not looking back at me. Granny, you said that Mum had forgotten how to be an Indian, that she would learn. She didn't, did she? But me and Brother learned plenty. How to live with a drunk for a mother. How many drinks it takes before you pass out. How to avoid your mother when she has a hangover. How to smooth things over so no one remembers anything. How to clean up after her. How to hope that maybe this night your mother will stay home. Granny, my mother didn't forget how to be an Indian, she *was* being an Indian!

The heron fluttered, its feathers brushing against the woman's wet cheek. She inhaled the scent of the bird—the smell of marsh water, reeds, and fish. The bird remained silent, an almost calm look in its eyes. Without wanting to, the woman remembered a day when their mother had washed and braided her and Brother's hair. Mum sang a song, "Fly Me to the Moon." She said she had the most beautiful children, and that their hair was the tenth wonder of the world. Brother and Sister laughed in each other's faces and sang along with their mother.

The woman touched her hair, remembering the feel of her mother's hands as she drew the brush through the long mass of hair, then held the strands as she began the braids. Her mother's hair had been black, pulled into a ponytail or left falling down her back when she went out.

The smell of the bird reminded the woman of how she had loved it here as a child. Grampa taking her and Brother fishing, their lines getting tangled in the pickerel weed. Brother getting so excited he'd cry out, "Fish, fish, come and jump on my hook. I want to eat you!" The terns circling above them, their raucous voices begging for a piece of whatever the trio might catch. Marsh wrens clattering as they delicately flew from reed to cattail. Red-wings whistling and giving chase to anything that threatened their nests. Grampa paddling further into the channels where everything was quiet except for the startled croak of a heron or an egret. They would sit for hours, fishing and growing sleepy under the sun, Grampa's voice telling stories.

Brother never stopped loving it here. But he was different. Even from the start, Brother was marked in some way. His way of seeing, his dreams, the way he would listen, as if he heard something that no one else could hear. Oh yes, Granny, the special brother and the sister who was going to grow up to be like her mum. Isn't that the way it was? I've missed you so much, Granny. I would call you on the phone and hear your voice and want to rush back to you. But I couldn't come back here. Not here. I'm lonely, Granny. I have no children, I wouldn't have children. I was afraid to. I'm lonely. I go to my job, I come home, I eat, I watch TV, I go to sleep. I dream. You told me that when we dream our souls fly. My soul doesn't fly, Granny. It's a lead sinker that pulls me down till I can't breathe and I wake up crying and afraid. You told us lies, Granny. Standing at the cookstove, putting together the stew, you told us we were a proud people. Brother believed you. *He* stayed here to keep himself an Indian. As if living in a run-down shack on a god-forsaken island is something special, something the whites don't have, something that makes us better than them. What a joke. Proud people. Proud people? Drunks! What a lie, Granny. Isn't it?

The heron moved. Its eyes looked again into the woman's eyes. Its feathers rustled in her arms. The scent of the marsh brought another memory. Granny laughing as she mended some clothes and Mum sitting next to her making a pair of earrings for her daughter. There hadn't been enough red beads and Mum had to start all over again so the pattern would be consistent and perfect. The girl watched her mother patiently threading the beads, the kerosene lamp hanging over her mother's head, casting lights on her fingers as she slowly beaded the earrings and talked with Granny. Brother sat in the corner of the room reading books. Looking up from the page, he smiled at his sister.

*Come home.*

The words hung in the air like the Harvest Moon. The woman stared into the eyes of the heron, seeing her reflection and something more. What was it? The bird stared back steadily and clearly.

What do I have to come home to? What happened, Granny? I never thought you'd die. I wished and wished for Mum to die when she was drunk. Then she did. I didn't mean it! I was always scared. Scared of the screaming and shouting when she got drunk. Scared of the men she hung around with. Scared to see her go out. Brother was scared too. He would hold me and tell me I couldn't change her, couldn't make her different. I knew he was right, but I was a little kid and part of me thought that if I wished hard enough, she would stop drinking. Then I began to wish she would die. And that wish came true. Why couldn't the other one? I'm afraid of death, Granny. I'm afraid of life. I look in the mirror and see my mother's face. I haven't touched a drop in five years, yet here I am holding Heron and wanting to feel the hot taste of whiskey in my mouth.

I'm scared without you, Granny. Even living in the city, I knew you were here for me. I could call you and hear your voice. You told me you were proud of me for not drinking. That you prayed for me. That you missed me, but you knew I was doing what I had to do. I am so scared! You held us when Mum couldn't. You talked to us when she couldn't. You yelled at her only once when you told her she was making shame in the Creator's sight. She laughed at you, but then she cried. She pointed at me: "Don't let her be like me. Don't let Marie be like me!" Granny, I remember how you tried to pull her into your arms, but she ran out of the door, hair still matted from the night's sleep, her makeup smeared and dissolving. She ran out the door and came back dead. I didn't mean it!

*Come home.*

The heron's heart was beating, erratic and small against Marie's fingers. She rubbed her wet face on the feathers and touched the beak. The bird shifted, its weight falling more on her. The eyes regarded her, the moon's reflection staring out at her. Her own face looking out at her. Her mother's face looking out at her.

*Come home.*

I thought if I left this island I could save myself. But I gave up parts of me at the same time. I'm lonely, Granny. Lonely for the smell of the water, the way the sky looks when it's going to rain, the men setting trap lines in the fall, the way the water looks in the winter, hundreds of muskrat houses poking up through the marsh, the sound of Brother's laughter. You and Grampa. My mother. My mother who stares out of the mirror.

*Come home.*

The words floated above Marie's head, above the heron's head. She could touch them, if only she reached for them. Heron's eyes held hers, almost like an embrace.

The last time I saw a heron was five years ago. I saw one sitting in a willow tree as I left the house and was driving toward the road that would take me over the bridge and into the city. I laughed when I saw it. It was so big and awkward perching on a willow branch. When I got closer, the heron squawked and flew out of the tree. I stopped the car and watched, the graceful legs floating behind its body, like strings across the sky. I watched until the blue wings disappeared over the marsh. I thought for a moment that you had sent the bird, Granny. I went away from here because I thought I wasn't strong enough to be like you. I thought I wasn't strong enough to stay. I ran away from you, from my mother. Forgive me, Granny. Forgive me, Mum.

*Come home.*

The words became the heron's low croak. The bird shuddered in Marie's arms—the eyes, the powerful eyes, never leaving Marie's own. The bird's heart stopped beneath Marie's fingers. The moon's light intensified as it focused on the pair sitting in the road.

Marie lay the bird aside and went to open the trunk of the car. She got out the tire iron, the only thing she had to dig a grave. She fought the hard dirt, scooping and struggling to make a shallow hole. She picked up the bird, once again breathing in the smell of the island. She laid the heron into the earth and plucked a few of the feathers. She covered the grave with dirt and reeds. She touched the grave and looked at the moon. The moon looked back, its light caressing her face.

Six more miles to Granny, and to Brother, who would be holding out his hands to her, standing in the open doorway. Beyond him would be Granny, waiting to be washed and covered with sweetgrass. They would tend her together and sing for her. There would be food to prepare and drummers to call.

"I'm coming, Granny."

Clutching Heron's feathers in her hand, Marie put the car in gear and headed up the road.

# This Place

"Mother, I am gay. I have AIDS." The telephone call that it almost killed him to make.

The silence. Then, "Come home to us."

David came home because he was dying. He expected to see his place of birth in a new way, as if he were a photographer capturing scenes through diverse lenses. *Scene one: through a living man's eyes. Scene Two: through a dying man's eyes.* But the beauty remembered was the beauty that still existed. Nothing had changed in ten years. The water of the Bay just as blue and smooth. The white pines just as tall and green. The dirt roads as brown and rutted as the day he had left. His mother as small and beautiful, her dark hair with even more grey streaks running through the braid she wrapped around her head.

Had nothing changed but him?

He had left this place and gone to the city to look for other men like himself. He found them. He found a new life, a different life. He found so much. Even the virus that now ate at him. David came home and was afraid of death.

David could feel the virus changing his body, making marks on his insides. Outside, too, his body was marked: by the tumors growing on his face and the paleness of his skin. He worried that the virus was somehow taking away his color, bleaching the melanin that turned him polished copper in the summer and left him light terra cotta in winter. He could feel the virus at war with the melanin and he could not check the battle. He couldn't hold this virus in his fist and squeeze the death out of it. He could only wait and look in the mirror to see the casualty of this war. David was afraid.

"Mother, am I turning white?"

"No, my baby son. You are dark and beautiful. Your hair is black and shiny as ever. Your eyes are tired, but still as brown and strong as the day you left this place."

He knew she lied to him. Mothers lie about their children's pain. *It will go away,* they say. *I'll make it better,* they say. *Oh, Mother, make it better, make it go away. I'm afraid of death.*

He felt the virus eating his hair. It fell out in clumps as he combed it. His forehead got broader and receded further. The blackness of the strands had dulled to some nondescript color. His braid was thin and lifeless, not as it used to be, snapping like a whip across his back, or gliding down his back like a snake.

David's sister brought her children to see him. They crawled on his lap and kissed him. He was afraid for them. Afraid the virus would reach out of his body and grab these babies and eat at them until they, too, disappeared in its grip. The virus put a fear in him—a fear that he could wipe out his people by breathing, by talking, by living. David saw, in his dreams, the virus eating away at this place until it was gone.

His dreams were also about a place called death. Death seemed to be a gaping hole in the world where David looked and there was nothing. He would wake from these dreams sweating, his limbs filled with pain. He had lived his life so well, so hard, clutching it to him like food, swallowing and being nourished. He wanted to greet death like that, opening his arms to it, laughing and embracing that other world. But he was afraid.

"Mother, I am afraid of death."

"Joseph is coming to visit."

On a day when David was seated in his chair before the window, looking out at the way the bright sun had turned everything in the yard golden, he heard the pickup truck making its way down the dirt road to the house. He also heard a voice singing. David laughed out loud. The song being sung was "All My Exes Live in Texas," and he knew that Joseph was on his way to him.

The truck came to a screeching, convulsive stop. David's mother went out to greet the man who jumped from the truck laughing, "Where's the patient?" As David watched, Joseph extracted a brown paper bag and an orange-striped cat from the truck. "Meet my friend, the Prophet. You can call her Prophet." David's mother reached for the cat who nudged at her breast and looked into her face. Joseph kissed Grace on the cheek. Prophet licked Grace's face. David wondered at the fact that Joseph looked the same as he had when David was a child. Dressed in faded jeans and a flannel shirt, Joseph's face was lean and unlined. His nose was sharp and slightly curved at the end, like a bird's beak. His eyes were black and round, reminding David again of a bird, perhaps a kestrel or a falcon. Joseph wore long, beaded earrings that draped across the front of his shirt. His hair, black and coarse, was tied back with a leather string. His fingers were covered with silver-and-garnet-studded rings, his hands delicate but used. Joseph looked at the young man in the window and lifted his hand in a greeting. Then he smiled and his face took on the unfinished look of a child. David waved back, feeling excitement—the way he used to feel before going to a party.

"This ain't goin' to be like any party you ever went to," Joseph remarked as he stepped through the doorway. "Here, have a Prophet," and he lifted the orange cat from Grace's arms onto David's lap.

Prophet looked intently at David's face, then kneaded his lap and settled herself on it, where she purred. David stroked the orange fur and scratched the cat's head. She burrowed deeper in his lap. "I would get up to greet you, but I think Prophet's got something else in mind."

Joseph laughed. "We wouldn't want to disturb her highness. David, we have not seen each other in many years." He bent down to kiss the young man on his forehead. "You don't look so good." Joseph eyed him critically.

"Thanks. But you look the same as ever."

"You in a lot of pain," Joseph said in a statement, not a question.

"Yeah, a lot of pain. I take about fifty pills a day. They don't seem to make that much of a difference." David continued to stroke Prophet.

"You think I can cure you?"

"No."

"Good, because I can't. All of us are afraid of death, though. We don't know what to expect, what to take with us." He looked in his paper sack. "Maybe I got the right things here."

Grace went into the kitchen, and Joseph pulled up a chair and sat beside David. Looking at Prophet asleep on David's lap, Joseph remarked, "Cats is smart. This one had a brother looked just like her. I called him Tecumseh. One morning I woke up and he was gone. I asked the Prophet if she knew where her brother went. She looked at me and blinked, then turned her head away like I'd said somethin' rude. I went outside to look for Tecumseh and I found him, layin' dead under a rose bush. It was a good year for the roses, they was bloomin' to beat the band. He had chosen the red roses to die under. That was a good choice, don't you think? I buried him under that red rose bush. The old man knew what *he* wanted, but he had to let me know, me not bein' as smart as a cat. Prophet came out and sat on the grave. She sat there for three days and nights. Cats are different from us. We worry about fittin' things to our own purpose. Cats don't worry about them things. They live, they die. They get buried under a red rose bush. Smart, huh?"

"You got any spare rose bushes? Only make mine flaming pink!" David laughed, then began coughing, blood spattering the kleenex he held to his mouth.

The Prophet jumped from David's lap and sat on the floor, her back to him.

"Now I've done it," David gasped. "Come back. Here kitty, kitty, kitty."

The Prophet turned and gave him a look of contempt, her back twitching, her tail moving back and forth on the floor.

"Huh," Joseph said. "She ain't comin' back for a while. Don't like the name Kitty."

Grace came in to announce dinner. David grabbed his cane and shuffled to the table. He sat down, gasping for breath. "Takes longer every time. I think I'm losing feeling in my right leg, but what the hell, I'd crawl to the table for Mother's beef stew." He half-heartedly lifted the spoon to his mouth. "My appetite's still pretty good, isn't it, Mother?"

Grace smiled at her son. "The day your appetite goes is the day I go."

She had made fresh bread to eat with the stew and set dishes of pickles and cheese on the table. Joseph rubbed his hands together in glee. "This looks good!" They ate, talking local gossip, the Prophet sitting daintily beside Joseph's chair. David's hands shook as he barely fed himself, spilling stew on his blue shirt. Grace fussed and tied a napkin around his neck. David smiled, "Next, she'll be feeding me or giving me a bottle." He winked at his mother and blew a kiss across the table to her. She caught it and put it on her cheek.

Joseph watched while he fed bits of meat to Prophet. He looked in his sack and pulled out a dish covered in waxed paper. "I made these this mornin'. Butter tarts. The flakiest crust you'll find anywhere. You gotta use lard, none of that shortenin'. Lard is what makes a crust that'll melt in your mouth. It's my gift to you, David."

As David bit into the sweetness of the tart, he looked at Joseph, his earrings swinging against his shoulders, his hands making patterns in the air as he described the making of the tarts, and David thought, *He acts like a queen.* He looked harder at Joseph, thinking, if you put him in a city, in a gay bar, the old nelly would fit right in. David laughed out loud.

Grace looked startled, but Joseph grinned and nodded his head. "Catchin' on, my young friend?"

As he helped clear the table, David smiled with his new knowledge. Collapsing into his reclining chair, David swallowed his medicine and laid his head back, closing his eyes. He could hear the murmurs between Joseph and Grace, his mother always a living, vivid presence in his life—his reason for hanging on so long to life. "I love you, Mother," he whispered. He opened his eyes to the dry touch of Joseph's fingers on his face. His mother was bringing out the moccasins she had made from rabbit hide and had beaded the nights they sat and watched TV. She presented them to Joseph. He unlaced his red hightops and slipped the beautiful moccasins on his feet. He put his feet out in front of him in admiration. He got up and walked in them. He jumped and clicked his heels together. "Thank you, Grace. You haven't lost your touch, have you? Now it's time for you to go. Don't come back till the mornin'."

Grace gathered her things together and stood looking at David. Her face shifted with emotions: sorrow, pride, fear, love. She kissed her son and hugged Joseph. They watched her leave.

Joseph turned and asked David, "You tryin' to be brave for your mom? Let me tell you somethin' about mothers. They know everything. She feels what you're goin' through. Can't hide it, even though you try."

"No! I don't want her to know how bad it gets. I can see it in her face, she gets crazy not knowing what to do for me. But this is the real crazy part, I don't want to let go of her. That death . . . that place. . . she won't be there."

The Prophet jumped on Joseph's lap and began washing herself. "That's true. Her time isn't here yet. David, you have lived your life in the way that was best for you. You think Grace didn't know why you left here? Think she didn't know you was gay? You can't tell someone like Grace not to go crazy when her son is dyin'. You can't tell her how to mourn you. And you can't be draggin' her along with you when you leave this place."

"I don't want to do that. I feel like a little kid when I was scared of a nightmare. Mother would make it go away. Death is like that nightmare. I gotta meet it on my own, but I'm scared."

"Yes, I know you are," and Joseph reached for David's hand. David's bony fingers closed over Joseph's.

"When I lived in the city, I used to get so homesick for this place. I'd picture the way it looked—the sky, the trees, my relatives. I'd dream it all up in my mind, but I never thought I would come back.

I made my life in the city, thinking that I couldn't come back here. My people don't want queers, faggots living among them. But now, some of us are coming home to die. Where else would we go but back to our homes, our families? What a joke, eh? They couldn't deal with my life, now they gotta deal with my death. God, I think about the guys that really can't go home. They have to die alone in some hospital, or even on the street. There was guy I knew, Ojibwe, and he died outside his apartment. I heard about it after it happened and I got in this rage! People just walking by him, probably thinking, oh here's another drunk Indian, just walking by him! And him, getting cold and no one would touch him." Tears were moving down David's face. He lifted his hand to wipe his face. "That's when I hated being an Indian. My own people, hateful to that guy. He was scared to go home. Probably thought they'd throw him out again, or stone him or something."

"Well, Indians got no immunity from hatefulness or stupidity, David. Maybe he had made his choice to die alone. Maybe he didn't have a home to go to."

David looked shocked. "No, that can't be true. I know what it's like. I grew up here, remember? It seemed like I had to make a choice, be gay or be an Indian. Some choice, eh? So I moved to the city." David sighed, then began to cough.

Joseph stroked Prophet, whose ears were twitching. "Even a city can't take the Indian part away. Even a virus can't do that, my young friend." He dipped into his sack and held out a piece of metal to David. "Look in this. What do you see?"

David held the piece of metal to his face. He saw a blurred image of himself, tumors covering his face. When he tilted the piece of tin, he saw himself laughing and dressed in his finest clothes, dancing in the bar in the city. He tilted it yet another way and saw himself dancing at a pow wow, his hair fanning out as he twirled and jumped. In another tilt, he saw himself as a child, sitting on Grandmother's lap.

"Which one is you?" Joseph asked.

"All of them."

"When the Prophet was a kitten," Joseph said, petting the now sleeping cat, "she used to keep me awake at night. She'd jump on my head just as I was dozin' off. I'd knock her away and turn over, but just when that sweet moment of sleep was callin' me, she'd jump on my head again. I thought maybe she was hungry and I'd get up to feed her. She'd eat, then start the whole routine all over again. She even got Tecumseh in the act. While she'd jump on my head, he'd get under the covers and bite my feet. I finally gave up and got out of bed and went outside and looked at the sky. About the fifth night of these carryin' ons, I *really* looked at the sky. I saw all the stars as if they was printed on the insides of my eyes. I saw the moon like she really was. And I started to pray to Sky Woman, blinkin' and shinin' up there. She answered me back, too, all because the cats was smarter than me. Nothin' hides in front of old Sky Woman. You might think *she's* hidin' when you can't see her, but she's there, checkin' everything out. People can't hide from her. And people can't hide from themselves."

"Is that what I've done?" David asked, his face sad. "I've always been proud of being Mohawk, of being from here. I *am* proud of being gay even though everywhere I turned, someone was telling me not to be either. In the city they didn't want me to be Native. In this place, they don't want me to be gay. It can drive you crazy! *Be this. Be that. Don't be this way.* So you get to be like an actor, changing roles and faces to please somebody out there who hates your guts for what you are." David laughed. "When I was diagnosed I thought, well, now I don't have to pretend anymore. It's all out in the open. I'm going to die, and why did I waste my time and tears worrying about all this other stuff? I got real active in AIDS work. I wanted to reach out to all the Indian gays I knew, form support groups, lean on each other. 'Cause the other guys just didn't understand us. I was a fireball for two years, real busy, but then I got too sick to do much of anything. My friends were good, but they couldn't take care of me anymore. I came home. Here I sit, Grandfather, waiting for death, but scared shitless."

Joseph began to hum and sing, "Crazy. . . I'm crazy for feelin' so lonely." He stuck his hand inside the sack and handed David a piece of paper.

*We, as the original inhabitants of this country, and sovereigns of the soil, look upon ourselves as equally independent and free as any other nation or nations. This country was given to us by the Great Spirit above; we wish to enjoy it, and have our passage along the lake, within the line we have pointed out. The great exertions we have made, for this number of years, to accomplish a peace and have not been able to obtain it; our patience, as we have observed, is exhausted. We, therefore, throw ourselves under the protection of the Great Spirit above, who will order all things for the best. We have told you our patience is worn out, but that we wish for peace and whenever we hear that pleasing sound, we shall pay attention to it. Until then, you will pay attention to us.*

"My ancestor. Quite a man." David held the paper in his thin hands.

"Yes, he was. Diplomats, they called him and his sister. We call them warriors."

David read the words again. "Grandfather, I would like to be a warrior like this man. I would like to see death coming and run to meet it, not afraid, not hiding behind my mother."

"Who says you ain't a warrior? David, the bravest people I knew were the ones that lived and kept on livin'. Those two, Tyendinaga and Molly, they fought to keep us alive as a people. Looks to me like you're as fine a warrior as they was. David, you lived!"

The Prophet suddenly came awake and stretched to her full length. She sat up and washed her face. She blinked at David, her yellow eyes staring at him until he looked away. She jumped off Joseph's lap and settled herself in front of David's feet.

"Trust the Prophet to interrupt the proceedings. Let's go outside and sit on the porch." Joseph stood up and stretched his arms and shook his legs.

David reached for his cane, his body curved and stooped. Joseph got a blanket to wrap him in against the cool night air. David made his way toward the front door. Joseph went to the kitchen and brought out two mugs of coffee and the rest of the butter tarts. They settled on the porch steps.

"David, look at the moon. When she's a crescent like that, I think Sky Woman's smilin' at us. More than likely, laughin'. She has big jobs to do like pullin' in the tides, and we sit here yappin' about life and death."

"The moon is beautiful. Somehow, it never seemed to shine like that in the city." David began coughing again, his body shaking and throbbing.

Joseph held onto him until the shaking stopped. "David, you're just a rez boy, ain't you? Nothin' looks as good as here, eh? But I think so too. One time, a long time ago, I thought about leavin' here."

"Why didn't you? It can't have been easy for you. Or were things different then? Maybe not so homophobic, not so much hatred?"

"Oh, things was bad. But not in that way. There was hatred, alright. The kind that makes people turn to the bottle or put a gun in their mouth and shoot." David winced, remembering his father's death. Joseph continued. "That kind of hatred, self-hatred. I stayed because I was supposed to. I fought it, but I had to stay. It was my job." He began a song. *"Your cheatin' heart will tell on you. You'll cry and cry, the way I do.* Sing with me, David." And they sang until the last words were finished and Joseph hugged David.

"I thought medicine men were supposed to chant and cast spells, not sing old Hank Williams' songs," David teased.

Joseph looked surprised. "Oh, some do. Some do. But how many medicine people you know, David?"

"Only you, Grandfather."

"Well then, there you go. What you see is what you get."

"When my father died, I remember being shut out from what was going on. I know they were all trying to protect me and Sister, but we were scared. One day he was there, the next day he wasn't.

He wasn't the greatest dad, but he was ours! You were there, Grandfather. Why did he do it?"

Joseph took a deep breath and let it out. It lingered in the night air like a puff of smoke. "Because he didn't know any other way. Are you judgin' him, David? 'Cause if you are, you can forget it. Too many people made a judgment on your father all his life. He doesn't need yours to add to it." Joseph's face became angry, then softened as he took David's hand again. "Children get scared. We fail you because we fail ourselves. We think *you'll* get over it because you're younger and have fewer memories. Grownups are fools, David. Your father didn't know what else to do with his life, a life he thought was worthless. So he shot it away."

David wept. "I've thought about shooting mine away, like him. Like father, like son, isn't that what the people would say? So, I didn't, all because I didn't want to be mentioned in the same breath with him. Pride, that's all that kept me going. And I couldn't do the same thing to my mother and sister that he did to us."

"You're a lot like your dad. Sweet, like he was. Oh yes," Joseph looked at David's disbelieving face, "a sweet man. When we was at residential school together, he's the one that took me under his wing. He fought the grownups and the other kids that ganged up on me. He was always my friend. He didn't fail me, ever. And I tried not to let him down, but I wasn't enough to keep that gun out of his hand. Nobody was enough, David. Not you, or your mom or your sister. Don't you judge him. He wouldn't have judged you." Joseph raised his face to the crescent moon and closed his eyes.

David felt a small piece of pain dislodge from inside him. It floated away in the night's darkness. "Thank you for telling me that, Grandfather. I always loved him."

Joseph smiled, his crooked teeth shining white in the moon's light. "Love is a funny thing, David. It stays constant, like her," he pointed to the crescent. "When you cut through all the crap, the need and greed part, you got the good, lastin' stuff. She knew that," and he pointed again to the moon. "She put herself up there to remind us of her love, not to admire her pretty shine. Of course, the pretty shine doesn't hurt, does it?" And they laughed together.

David said, "I met my pretty shine in the city. He will always be the love of my life, even though he doesn't feel that way about me. We're still friends. . . . God, the city was so different for me—I loved it! Excitement. All those gorgeous men. If I'd stayed here, I wouldn't have known the world was full of gay people. If I'd stayed here though, maybe I wouldn't have gotten AIDS." David pulled the blanket closer around himself and shivered.

Joseph squeezed David's wasting fingers. "Do you regret any of it?"

"No. I've thought about that a lot. I only wish I could have stayed, but I thought I had to make the choice and don't know what would have happened if I hadn't left."

Joseph rustled in his sack. "Who can read the future? Well, maybe I can, but can you read the past as well? Here, take this."

David held out his hand. A dry snakeskin was deposited into his dry palm. The skin was faded but still showed orange-and-black markings.

"I saw this snake shed her skin. I was walking in the bush and heard a very small noise. I watched her wriggle out of her old life, just like she was removin' an overcoat. It took this snake a long time, but then, there she was in her new overcoat, her old skin just lyin' there waitin' for me to pick it up and give it to you."

"Thank you, Grandfather. It's beautiful." David touched the snakeskin and looked into Joseph's face. "I think it would be wonderful if we could shed ourselves like this and have a brand-new, beautiful skin to face the world. Or maybe, to face death."

"We do, David. A snake doesn't put on a new skin with different colors. She has the same one, just layers of it. She doesn't become a new snake, but older and wiser with each shedding. Humans shed. We don't pay attention to it, though. We get new chances all the time. A snake makes use of her chances; that's why she's a snake and we're not. We never know when we got a good thing goin'."

"That's true! Mother used to tell me I was lucky, I had it good compared to other little boys. She was right, of course." David giggled into his hand. "She is always right. Why is that, Grandfather?"

"Now you got me. That's something I'll never know either!"

They laughed, the sound filling the night air. Prophet scratched at the door to be let out. "The Prophet's afraid she's missin' out on something. Those butter tarts, maybe." Joseph got up to open the door.

The Prophet streaked out the open door and ran to the cluster of apple trees. She climbed one and sat on a branch. David could see the yellow glow of her eyes as she watched the men drink their coffee and bite into the tarts.

Joseph remarked between bites, "Prophet does it every time. I'd sit around all night talkin' if she didn't remind me why I was here."

David started to shake. "I'm afraid, Grandfather."

"Yes, I know, David. We'll go inside, and you can lay down while I make some special tea. I'm here with you, David. I won't leave you."

David clutched the snakeskin in his hand and struggled to his feet. He made his way into the house and to the couch where he started coughing and spitting up blood. Joseph cleaned David's face and wrapped the blanket tightly around his skinny body. He went to the kitchen, and David could hear him singing, "I fall to pieces . . . each time I see you again." David smiled, the voice reassuring to him.

"The Prophet's still in that apple tree, starin' at the house," said Joseph, as he brought a steaming mug of liquid to David.

David sipped the tea and made a face. "What is this stuff? It tastes like wet leaves!"

"It is wet leaves. Drink up. It's good for what ails you."

"Yeah, right," David smiled, "I notice you're not drinking any."

"Well, I'm not the sick one, am I?"

David drank the brew, watching Joseph walk around the room, picking up books and stacking them neatly, straightening a picture hanging on the wall, tidying a lamp table. "There's a dust rag in the broom closet. The rug could use a shake and the windows need a wash," David said teasingly.

"You're a regular Henny Youngman, ain't you?"

"Who?"

"All finished?" Joseph pointed to the mug. "If you want more, you can't have it. I only brought enough for one cup."

David pushed the mug toward Joseph. "Please, no more. I think I'll survive without it."

"Ah, survival. Let me tell you about that one." Joseph sat on the couch at David's feet.

David felt heavy in his body. He tried to lift his hand, but it was too much of an effort. He tried to speak, but his voice wouldn't move out of him. He looked at Joseph who was talking, but his voice was thin and far away. He saw that Prophet had come back into the house and was sitting on Joseph's lap. The Prophet stared at David with her yellow eyes and smiled at him. Was that a smile? What was that tea? Wet leaves. . .and David was falling was falling back into wet leaves and it was autumn the air smelled like winter he was a boy a boy who jumped up from wet leaves and ran he ran he was chasing something he felt so good so good this is what childhood is you run you laugh you open your mouth you feel the wind on your tongue the sun on your head the apple trees were giving up their gifts of fruit you picked an apple you feel you taste the juice running down your throat the apple made a loud crunch as you bit and the swallows in the tree were waiting for the core to be thrown down so they could share the fruit of the tree the geese were flying you ran you ran into the cornfield and scared the pheasant who was picking at the seed you laughed you laughed it was a perfect day you picked up a feather and put it in your pocket the day was perfect when you were a child you ran you laughed you played you were loved you loved you were a child it was good so good good to be a child in this place this place this place never changed this place this place.

David opened his eyes. The Prophet was washing her tail. Joseph held a turtle rattle in his left hand. He was talking . . . *and then the church people sent their missionaries here to teach us to be christian but we. . .*

David was falling he fell into the sound of the turtle's rattle he fell into the turtle's mouth he shook his body shook and . . . *fought them*. . . he fell into the sound of the rattle he was the rattle's sound the music the music he was dancing dancing with the first man he ever loved they were dancing holding holding the music the music the turtle's music was in them through them in them . . . *killed us*. . . he went home he went with the first man he ever loved the music was beating was beating their hearts the rattle the music they fell onto the bed the music the music touched them the turtle touched them the rattle touched them they touched they touched the touching was music was music his body singing music his body the rattle of the turtle the first man he loved . . . *we fought back*. . . their bodies singing shaking joining joining everything was music was music so good so good good the first man he loved Thomas Thomas . . . *they kept killing us off*. . . Tommy Tommy singing sighing joining . . . *but we*. . . singing our bodies singing Tommy David Tommy Tommy . . . *survived*. . . .

David's eyes opened. The room was dark. The Prophet was staring, smiling, her eyes brilliant yellow. Joseph was staring also, his eyes sending out shafts of brilliance, laser beams into his soul.

"Grandfather."

Joseph held up the rattle and sang a song with no words, a song in a high, quivering voice. Joseph's face changed shape. He became a cat. The Prophet sat smiling, her teeth white in the dark room. Joseph sang and became a wolf, lemon-yellow eyes steady on David. Joseph sang and he became a snake hissing his song, his eyes sending out shards of light. Joseph sang and shook the turtle. He sang.

"Grandfather."

David was falling he fell into the song of the cat the song of the wolf the song of the snake the song of the turtle he fell he fell into the turtle's mouth the turtle's song he was shaking was shaking his grandmother was singing was singing a song a song in Indian his grandmother was singing singing he was singing with Grandmother he was sitting on Grandma's lap her lap she was holding him close so close . . . *our people survived*. . . she sang his mother sang his sister sang his father sang he sang he was singing in Indian Indian the voices the songs in Indian . . . *the sicknesses came*. . . singing

singing his grandmother holding him his mother his father singing . . . *measles, smallpox*. . . Grandmother talking singing in Indian the language the song of Indian the people the song Grandma's hair brushing against his face as she whispered and told him he . . . *AIDS*. . . was an Indian Indian Mohawk singing songs Mohawk the voices Kanienka 'ha'ka the song the song of this place this Indian place this place.

The rattle was silent. The Prophet was sitting in a hump, the fur around her neck electric, like an orange ruff. Joseph sat, his laser eyes bright in the face of an old, old man. He spoke, his voice not audible, the words not recognizable, and David heard.

"They took parts of us and cut them up and threw them to the winds. They made lies we would believe. We look for the parts to put ourselves back together. To put the earth back together. It is broken. We look for truth to put us all together again. There is a piece here. A part there. We scavenge and collect. Some pieces are lost. We will find them. Some parts are found, and we do not see them yet. We gather the pieces and bring them together. *We* bring them together. *We* make the truth about ourselves. *We* make the truth."

David was falling was falling he fell he fell into the sound of the ancient voice the ancient words he was falling into the sounds of screaming screaming in his face dirty Indian faggot fucking faggot the voices screaming you dirty Indian you the sound of fists of fists the sound of hate the sound of hate you dirty Indian you dirty faggot the sound of hate the sound of blood the taste of blood in his mouth the taste the hate the hate . . . *we collect the parts that have been damaged*. . . the hate the pain as they raped him you dirty Indian faggot the hate the blood the rape the sound of rape . . . *we hunt for the pieces*. . . the hate the pain the fear the dirty Indian faggot . . . *we gather it all together*. . . you filthy Indian scum you dirty you dirty you dirty . . . *we are resisters, warriors*. . . you dirty Indian you dirty faggot the rape the sound of you dirty filthy . . . *we do not believe the lies they*. . . the taste the taste the taste of hate in his mouth.

David cried out. Joseph stroked his thinning hair, the turtle held over his body. "They hurt us in so many ways. The least of what they did was to kill us. They turned us into missing parts. Until we find those missing parts we kill ourselves with shame, with fear, with hate. All those parts just waitin' to be gathered together to make us. *Us.* A whole people. The biggest missing piece is love, David. *Love!*"

The Prophet leapt in the air and hissed. She leapt again and knocked the turtle rattle back into Joseph's lap.

"The Prophet says we are not finished. Who am *I* to argue with *her?*"

David tugged at the man's arm. "Joseph. Grandfather. I am so thirsty, so thirsty."

David was falling was falling into the shake of the rattle he fell he fell into the turtle's mouth he fell he was flying he flew he was inside the turtle the turtle shook he fell into voices voices asking him are you ready his heart his heart was beating are you ready his heart grew larger his heart was beating his heart the turtle asked him are you ready his grandmother held out her hand and touched him are you ready are you ready his grandmother touched his heart are you ready his father touched his heart are you ready the people held out their hands are you ready he reached for their hands his heart was beating inside the turtle a drum a drum are you ready Turtle touched his heart are you ready he fell he put out his arms he held out his arms I am ready they touched him I am ready I am ready I am ready.

David opened his eyes. The taste of tears was in his mouth. "I saw it." Prophet jumped delicately on David's chest and licked the salt tears from his face. She sat back on her haunches and watched David speak. "I saw my grandmother, my father. They touched me." He began coughing again, retching blood.

Joseph held a towel to David's mouth and touched the young man's face. "You found your parts, your pieces." Digging into his sack, he pulled out a white feather. "This is from a whistling swan. They stop here in the spring before goin' on to Alaska. The thing about them—they never know what they'll find when they get there.

They just know they got to get there. When our bodies are no longer here, *we* are still here." He stood up, his joints creaking and snapping. "Your mother is comin'. The sun is real bright today. It's a good day to go." He scooped Prophet up from David's lap and draped her across his shoulder.

"Thank you, Grandfather," David whispered, his breath coming in ragged bursts.

David heard him go out the front door. He couldn't see, but he heard Joseph talking to the Prophet. He heard the truck door slam and the engine start its rattling and wheezing. David moved his hands on the blanket to find the tin, the snakeskin, his ancestor's words, the feather. He touched them and felt Joseph's presence. The sound of his mother's car made him struggle to sit up. He heard the door open and the footsteps of his mother coming into the room. He felt her standing by him, her cool fingers touching his face and hands.

He opened his mouth to say good-bye.

# Food & Spirits

*for my Dad*

Elijah Powless decided it was time to take a trip.

He was driven to the bus stop by his son and daughter-in-law who, at the last moment, asked again, "Are you sure you want to do this, Father?"

And for the tenth or twentieth time he answered, "I want to see my granddaughters in the city. They are women now, and before I die I want to see how they are doin'."

Daughter-in-law shook her head but refrained from saying the usual: "You're not going to die. You see the girls all the time when they come to visit." She just shook her head, worried about letting an eighty-year-old man ride on a bus for seven hours to go to a place he'd never been. A big city. A big city in the States. A big city with the reputation of being the murder capital of the world!

Elijah had no faith in what newspapers or TV knew about a city. His twin granddaughters lived there—that was enough for him to go on.

The twins, Alice and Annie, were thrilled but anxious about their grandfather's trip. They offered to pay for the train fare and had even investigated plane routes and prices, but Elijah was firm in his insistence on paying for the bus ride himself.

"I'll see more from a bus. It's October, it'll be real pretty to see the land from a bus window. Besides, I don't want the twins to put out their hard-earned money on my trip."

So the daughter-in-law and the son had dutifully packed the suitcase and said many prayers. Elijah had also determined that he would take a bag of whitefish, frozen and wrapped in newspaper, and a separate bag of fry bread because, as Elijah said, "They don't get this kind of food in Detroit. I'll just make sure they have enough to last a few days."

"Please be careful, Father," the daughter-in-law breathed in his ear as she hugged him good-bye.

Elijah promised to be careful, though he wondered what he would have to be careful of. He had lived a good life. He had survived residential school with his own language and esteem intact. He had survived the Great Depression with a wife and five children. He had nursed his wife through cancer and on to death. He'd lost two sons to the white world and the alcohol in it. His three remaining children had finished school, had gotten jobs. The son standing before him now was a carpenter in a union, had a good wife, had twin daughters who were a joy in Elijah's life. He had been sad when the twins moved to the States to work for the Indian Center there. He was surprised that they had left home, but the twins were surprising girls. They were women now, he reminded himself. Thirty years old, unmarried, and Annie had declared she was thinking about adopting a child. It would be nice, Elijah thought, to be a great-grandfather to Annie's child. That was partly the reason he was taking this trip. He had it in mind that those Natives down there would listen to a man like himself. In fact, he was sure of it.

Getting on the bus and finding a seat, he waved good-bye to his son and daughter-in-law. He remarked to the woman sitting next to him, "My children are unhappy that I'm taking a trip. They think I'm too old and I need to be careful."

The woman turned her wide, fresh face toward him and smiled. Her false teeth glowed. "These kids sure do like to worry, don't they? They can't imagine that we old-timers might want to have some fun too." She whispered to Elijah, "I'm going to Windsor to visit my boyfriend. My daughter is scandalized that a woman my age has a beau."

Elijah was scandalized too. "You are a handsome woman. How come you only got one?"

They were laughing as the bus pulled out of the terminal. Well, this is good, Elijah told himself. A good sign. Laughter at the beginning means laughter at the end.

Elijah was trying to figure out how the woman got her hair that shade of blue when she stuck out her hand. "My name is Shirley Abbott."

"Elijah Powless," he said, and shook her hand. "How'd you get your hair that shade of blue?"

Shirley put her hands up to her short, puffy hair. "It's a rinse. Supposed to bring out the highlights in white hair. Don't you like it?" Shirley looked worried.

"Oh yeah, I like it fine. Goes with your dress," and he pointed at the bright blue material. Shirley relaxed.

"I just retired from my job," Shirley said. "I was a schoolteacher. Powless. . . Powless. Is that a Mohawk name?"

"Yep. How'd you know?"

"My sister married a man from Six Nations. I guess I heard the name there. Maybe we're related!"

"Well, I never seen a Mohawk with blue hair, but then, I never seen a lot of things." Elijah shifted the sacks on his lap. "Whitefish from the Bay. You can't get this kind of fish in Detroit. I caught it myself. My twin granddaughters live there, in Detroit, but they don't fish. Too busy, I guess. And this fry bread was made by their mother." Taking a round slab out of the bag, he offered it to Shirley.

She took a bite and rolled her eyes heavenward to indicate her pleasure. "This is good bread, Elijah. My sister makes it, but not as good as this. You tell that daughter of yours that she is an excellent cook."

"She is a good cook. Guess you can tell," and he pointed to his round belly, straining against his white shirt. He had dressed very carefully for this trip. In addition to his white dress shirt, he had on the new brown corduroy pants with the cuff smartly turned up. He was wearing his turtle bolo tie and had gotten a fresh haircut just the day before. He ran his hand through his greying short hair. It felt good. He would look sharp for the twins.

He glanced at Shirley who was having a hard time keeping her eyes open. She smiled, "I guess I'll take a little nap. I was up most of the night, too excited to sleep."

"Well, you gotta be fresh for that boyfriend."

Shirley giggled and settled in her seat. She closed her eyes.

Elijah looked out the window. It was so pretty, the day. The trees were turning color, shedding their green and taking on red and gold. Elijah felt very content to be on this bus, riding to see his twins, looking out the window at the beautiful trees, the cornfields, the occasional hawk sitting on a fence post. The crows were having a good day in the fields. They swooped in a great body to scavenge among the corn.

Elijah looked around at the other passengers. He wondered where they were going, what they were going to do when they got there. "Curiosity killed the cat," his wife had always said. Elijah retorted that he wasn't a cat and *his* curiosity had kept him going this long. Edith. He missed her to this day. She was a good and pretty woman. The twins looked like her. That special look on their faces, a look of excitement, like each day was going to bring a surprise. Even when she was dying, Edith had that look on her face. Edith. Elijah fell asleep.

Elijah had a dream. He was getting off the bus and there was Annie, standing with a baby in her arms. Alice stood right alongside her holding another baby. He reached for the babies and they called out, "Great-grandfather!" He held the babies, and the twins said, "These are your great-grandchildren. Twins, like us!"

He woke up and looked at Shirley who was smiling at him.

"You must have had a pleasant dream. You were grinning and laughing like you got the present of your life."

"I did. I got twins from the twins."

As they traveled, Elijah and Shirley talked. He told her about

Edith. She told him about her husband, Alan.

"He wasn't good like your Edith. He was never happy with what he had. Always looking for some ship to come in. He gambled away almost every cent we had. I eventually got smart and put my earnings where he couldn't get to it. We did not have a peaceful life together. When he died, my daughter said, 'Good riddance.' I know what she meant, but it worried me that this was how she felt about her father."

"Takes more than a name to make a father. Kids don't get choices like grownups do. Mother, father, they gotta take what they get. If someone don't act like a father, why should a child love him like a daddy? You shouldn't worry about what's over. You got any grandchildren?"

Shirley shook her head no. "But my daughter is a lovely girl. She's given me a lot of pleasure in my life. I never had to worry about her for a minute."

Elijah nodded and looked out the window again. "Look, Shirley, there's a hawk comin' in on that tree! See how he hunches up and tucks his neck in? You'd never know he was there, would you? Hawks never give up. They'll chase something down till they get it. They gotta eat. None of this goin' to the store and gettin' food already there. Hawks gotta work."

"Can you picture a hawk going to the supermarket and picking out its food?" Shirley laughed.

"Well, now you mention it, I can't see it. If we worked as hard as the hawk for our food, we might think twice about throwin' so much away."

Shirley sighed, "I know what you mean, Elijah. These kids today, they don't know what it's like to go hungry. They think everything grows at the supermarket."

"Lots of kids know what it's like to go hungry. You just ain't been around them. Edie and me, we used to get the kids to help in the garden. I took 'em all huntin' and fishin'. But sometimes we went hungry too. But one thing, none of them is a waster of food."

"Look Elijah, there's the sign for Windsor!"

Shirley got up to go to the washroom. She came back smelling like lilac perfume, her lipstick newly applied, her blue hair stiff as a board.

Elijah made his way to the washroom and came back to his seat marveling at how small the room was. "I've never seen anything like it. While I was washing my hands I thought I was going to fall in the toilet, it was so crowded in there."

Shirley gathered her things together and sat, hands folded on top of her purse. "It's been a pleasure to meet you, Elijah. You tell those twins to take good care of you, now. I hope you enjoy your vacation."

Elijah thanked Shirley and helped her to her feet. He waved good-bye and watched her get off the bus to meet her beau.

Going through customs, Elijah wondered if Alice and Annie had changed much from six months ago when he'd last seen them. Riding through the tunnel that connected Detroit to Windsor, he smiled at his foolishness. They weren't children who changed constantly. They were women now, pretty much settled into what they would look and be like.

Elijah got up when the bus stopped. As he walked down the aisle, he caught glimpses of cement and traffic. Claiming his suitcase, he looked around for the twins. He went inside the terminal and still couldn't see them. He waited, suitcase by his feet, bags in hand, and watched all the people. There were so many kinds here. Black, brown, shades in between. White faces moved around him. They were walking to the bus, from the bus, sitting in the waiting room. Faces eating food, running after children, reading the papers. Teenage boys lined up at machines where they seemed to be playing some kind of game on a screen in front of them. Security guards and police walked through the building, keeping their eyes on the teenagers.

"Is this like TV?" Elijah asked a tall young man with dark brown skin. The young man was wearing a jacket with *Nike* streaking across the front. In fact, Nike seemed to be the young man's name, for the name was on his pants, on his shoes, and emblazoned on the cap that perched on his high hair.

"This ain't TV. It's Pacman, man."

"How does it work?"

"You puts the money in here, then you gotta get all the ghosts that pop up. Ain't you never seen this before? Man, where you been?"

Elijah dug in his pockets for coins.

"Hey man, you can't play with that kinda money. You needs American money." He looked at the old man and his disappointed face. "But here, don't worry none. See that place over there? You pays them some a your money and you gets back American. Here, I show you."

He took Elijah over to the booth that said American Exchange on its sign and showed him how to do it.

"Thank you, Nike. I should have done this before I left home. Too excited I guess. Excited about seein' my twin granddaughters. Maybe I'm gettin' old."

"Aw, don't worry about it. Hey, what you call me?"

"Nike."

The young man laughed, revealing a gap between his two front teeth. "My name ain't Nike. Anyways, it's Nik*eee*, not Nike. My name's Terrance. Terrance James," and he held out his hand for Elijah to shake. "Is somebody meetin' you? You shouldn't be wanderin' around, old man like yourself. What you got in them bags?"

"Whitefish from the Bay and some fry bread. Here, have a piece." Elijah pulled out a thick round and gave it to his new friend. "Sorry I got your name wrong. But how come you got that name on your clothes? Maybe you're wearin' somebody else's? My name's Elijah. Elijah Powless."

"No, man, these are my clothes. Nike's a brand name, like the company that makes 'em. You don't know that?" Terrance laughed. "Man, where you been?"

Elijah remarked as how he'd been in Tyendinaga and this was his first trip to Detroit and he wondered where his granddaughters were.

"That ain't right. Old man like yourself at the bus stop with nobody to meet him. That ain't right. You got a number for them girls? We could call them, tell them to get their butts over here to pick up their granddaddy. That ain't right."

Terrance pulled at his lip and looked worried while Elijah went through his pockets to find the number for the twins. "Here it is."

"There's the phone over there," Terrance pointed to the booth. "I'll wait here and play me some more games."

Elijah left his bags by Terrance, who assured him he'd keep an eye out for them. He dialed the number and let it ring ten times. He hung up the phone, wondering what to do next. Then he walked back.

"They ain't home," he said to Terrance. "I don't know what could be keepin' them, but I ain't worried. Now, show me how to play this game."

Terrance finished chewing the last piece of fry bread and showed Elijah where to put his quarters and how to play the Pacman game. "This is good bread. You got a whole bag of it? That all you got to eat?"

"No, I just brought it for the twins. You can't get this kinda food in Detroit. What kinda food *do* you get in Detroit?"

"Well, you can gets chicken or ribs or MacDonald's over there. But the best food is what my mama makes. Cornbread that'll melt in your mouth! Hey man, you Mexican or somethin'?" said Terrance, studying Elijah's face.

"I'm Mohawk. Indian."

"Yeah, we got somma them around here. They have a parade sometime. Me and my friends go. Somma them guys dance and wear these fancy costumes. Very impressive. My mama say that on my daddy's side, we gots Indian blood."

"Is that right? What kinda Indian? Is your daddy from around here?"

"My daddy ain't from around nowhere. He long dead and gone, I hopes. I don't know what kinda Indian. It's all the same," Terrance nodded sagely.

"Well, it ain't all the same. But then again," Elijah said, scratching his head, "maybe it is. You gotta point there, Terrance. You're a smart young man. You go to school?"

"Hell no! I ain't been in school for four years now. I quit when I was sixteen."

"Why'd you do that, a smart boy like yourself?"

"Hey man, I'm smart 'cause I ain't goin' to school. School ain't no place for Terrance James. Shit!"

"Maybe you were in the wrong school. Seems like you shoulda done real good in school." Elijah looked around the terminal. "I wonder where those twins are."

"What we gonna do, Elijah?"

"Play another game on this Pacman machine."

Terrance laughed and loaded up the quarters. They played three more games of Pacman before they noticed another man was making signals to Terrance. "I gotta go outside for a minute, Elijah. I'll tell you what. Across the street there's a bar. I know the dude who works there. They don't let you wait around here, unless you catchin' a bus. Why don't you go over there and wait. I be back here in a minute, just gotta little business to take care of. I'll wait on the twins and you can visit with Archibald. He the dude works across the street. It be alright there. He take care a you till them twins get here." Terrance shifted from one foot to the other.

"You in a hurry, Terrance? Here, take another piece of bread. I appreciate what you're doin'. Archibald, eh? I guess I am kinda thirsty. See you later."

Terrance smiled and hurried out after the man who was impatiently waiting.

Elijah stood for a few minutes, collecting his thoughts and belongings. He walked toward the door and looked out. There, across the street, just like Terrance said, was the place where he should go. FOOD & SPIRITS, the sign said.

He crossed the street, cars braking and horns blaring. A driver shouted out, "Watch where you're going, old man!"

Elijah waved and made it safely across the street and stood at the door where the FOOD & SPIRITS sign blinked on and off. He pushed on the door and went into the dark room. Music was playing from a jukebox in the corner. Two people turned to look at him when he entered the room.

Seeing the slim, dark man behind the bar, Elijah inquired, "Are you Archibald? Terrance James sent me here. Said you was a dude who'd look after me until my twins come to get me."

"I'm Archibald. What you want? What Terrance up to sendin' you here? I'll look after you, he say? Hummmpph." Archibald scratched his head, then continued to polish the glasses he had lined up in front of him.

"What does food and spirits mean? What kinda food you got here? What kinda spirits?" Elijah sat down on a stool, carefully placing his suitcase and parcels beside him.

Archibald polished the glasses, holding one up to the dim light, then polishing some more. "Just what it say. We got sandwiches, we got burgers, we got fries, we got drinks. What'll it be old-timer? And how'd you get my name from Terrance?" Archibald stared at Elijah. "Don't seem like nobody Terrance James would know."

"I met Terrance at the bus station. A smart young man. We played on the Pacman machine, and he told me his daddy was an Indian, like me."

"Hummmpph. What'll it be, old-timer?"

"Oh, I guess I'll have one a them pops. Ginger ale. I got some fry bread here. Have a piece."

Archibald looked suspiciously at the round hunk of bread offered to him. His brown eyes stared at Elijah. He shook his head no, his large Afro glinting from the light behind the bar. His dark brown skin reminded Elijah of the color of tea, nice and strong. Archibald's skin was smooth and unlined except for a scar running up his left eyebrow to his hairline. "One Vernor's comin' up."

He poured the ginger ale into a glass filled with ice. As he set it in front of Elijah he asked, "What kinda bread is that? Where you comin' from that you met Terrance at the bus? You waitin' on somebody?"

"This is fry bread, made by my daughter-in-law. I just come down from Tyendinaga. My twin granddaughters were supposed to meet me, but something seems to have held them up. Don't worry, they'll be here." Elijah took a long swallow from his glass. "Deeeelicious!"

"Oh, I ain't worryin'," Archibald stated. "It just seem you not the kinda man that Terrance would run with. Where's this Tidaga place?"

"Tyendinaga. It's an Indian place, very pretty. It's my home." He indicated the brown bag at his side. "I got whitefish here from the Bay. We eat a lot of it. I brought it for the twins 'cause they don't get this kinda food here."

"You got that right. You from a reservation, huh? I never met no Indian from a reservation. Give you a little rye to sweeten that ginger ale?"

Elijah held up his hands. "No, my drinkin' days are over. I'm eighty years old and stick with pop these days. So Archibald, my name is Elijah. Elijah Powless. What kinda spirits you got in this place?"

"Huh. The only kinda spirits what live here is whiskey spirit, gin spirit, and rum spirit. I'm pleased to meet you, Elijah." He held out his hand. "Maybe they be other spirits, too. I ain't taken inventory lately." Archibald laughed, and the woman sitting next to Elijah giggled.

"This here's Alana. Alana here's our spirit from the bus station. She hang out here when she ain't over there."

His eyes adjusted to the lack of light in the bar, Elijah turned to smile at the woman sitting next to him. She was smiling back, her bright pink lips opened over small, white teeth. Her skin was the color of unfinished pine, Elijah thought, and her hair was the blondest and curliest he'd ever seen. Curls were draped over her shoulders and tumbling down her back. She was wearing purple eye shadow that made her brown eyes look like wet silk. Two pinks spots, the size of half dollars, were painted on her cheeks. Her black skirt was very short and kept sliding up her legs, revealing purple garters around her thighs. Elijah looked away, lest Alana think him impolite to be staring at those purple garters.

"Hey, Elijah, how you doin'?" Alana held out her fingers for Elijah to touch. "So you a real Indian, Elijah? My, my, I never met one before. Imagine, in this bar, I be sittin' next to a real Indian. My, my."

Elijah shook Alana's fingers and offered her a piece of fry bread.

"This look like fry cake, don't it Archibald? Fry cake like my grandmama used to make." She took a bite, and her face expressed delight. "This is so good! Elijah, what you doin' carryin' sacks a fry cake around town? What's them twins thinkin' of, lettin' you wander 'round this city with a bag a fry cakes? It ain't safe!"

"It ain't their fault, Alana. I don't know what could have happened to them. But I ain't worried, yet. Do you know my twins, Alice and Annie? My granddaughters. Very pretty girls. They look like their grandmother, my Edie."

"How come Edie ain't with you, 'Lijah?" Archibald asked.

"Oh, she's been dead a long time. Cancer."

"Terrible," Alana whispered. "My mama had cancer. She had a lot of pain. I hope Edie didn't have no pain like that!"

"She did. But the place Edie's at now, I know she's happy there. No pain, just pretty things to see and all her relatives hangin' out there. Right before she died, she took my hand and said, 'Elijah, it's beautiful. It's beautiful.' Then she died. Edie was a pretty woman, so I can't imagine that the spirit place wouldn't be too."

"Ain't that beautiful," Alana sighed.

"How come Archibald said you was the spirit of the bus stop, Alana?"

"Oh him! He teasin' you," Alana giggled. "I ain't no spirit. Just a workin' girl. I work over at the bus stop sometime. I works here sometime."

"What do you do? I was a janitor when I was younger," Elijah took another sip from his glass.

Alana looked at Elijah, her silk eyes widening. "Honey, I just told you I was a workin' girl. I work the streets. Hustle. Workin' girl, workin' girl! I'm the spirit of the workin' girls!"

Archibald laughed, a rich baritone rumble coming through his throat. "Then I must be the spirit-keeper. The keeper of all the spirits in this here bar!"

Elijah looked at Archibald. "I like that. The spirit-keeper of the bar. It suits you. You look like the keeper of the spirits."

Archibald checked his reflection in the mirror behind the bar. "Well, maybe. But here, have another pop on me. Alana? Another of the same?" He busied himself with getting fresh napkins and clean glasses.

Alana checked her watch. "I guess I could stand another. It gettin' cold out there."

The door opened and a white man in a suit walked in. His eyes roamed around the bar and settled on the three faces looking at him. He turned around and went out the door.

Archibald laughed. "He don't like the color of the spirits in this here bar!" They laughed together, Alana's high-pitched giggle floating above them.

"What spirit are you, Elijah? If I'm the spirit of the workin' girl, and Archibald here's the spirit-keeper, then what are you?"

Elijah thought and took another swallow of his pop. "I guess you could call me the old Indian spirit. Put me up on the shelf with the whiskey spirits. I'll be the old Indian spirit."

They laughed, Archibald slapping his hand on the counter, Alana's pink cheeks moving and bobbing, Elijah's shoulders heaving and swaying.

"But still," Alana's voice was serious, "I read a book about Indians and they could see things. They had ceremonies and holy places. And they communicated with the other world." Alana shivered and pulled her rabbit coat up around her shoulders.

"Well, what's so unusual about that?" Elijah wanted to know. "It's just knowin' what to say and what to do when you meet up with somebody that ain't from your part of town."

"You got that right, 'Lijah," Archibald was nodding his head emphatically. "It happen all the time in here. Sometime I wonder if what I seen ain't from another world! And what I sees, my own eyes don't believe it!" He wiped the counter with his cloth.

Alana laughed, "Well, that true, that true. Some a my customers from another planet." She turned her face to Elijah. "But still, Indians *is* special. You all *see* things."

"We only see what's there. Nothin' special about that. But we've been around for a long time. This is our home, has been for millions of years. Guess you could say we're familiar with all that's around us. Your people didn't get the chance to be familiar yet. You was brought here without your say-so. We just always been here. It's different in the city, though. I worry about the twins. They don't fish, they don't get to see the hawks. I bet some days, they don't even see the sky!" He shook his head and took another sip.

Alana grabbed Elijah's hand. "But listen, Elijah, we got falcons livin' right here in the city. I seen it on the TV. They brought these here peregrine falcons to live on a tall buildin'. And they live there, and they had babies, right there on the ledge of that buildin'. Imagine that! Those big, ole birds livin' in this city. It ain't so bad here, if you just look up." Alana smoothed her blonde curls, lit a cigarette, and sipped her drink. "It ain't so bad here."

"I saw one a them birds once," Archibald remarked. "Didn't know what the hell it was! Thought it be some kinda vulture, flyin' down on me. Like to scare me to death. It flew down and grabbed a pigeon right off the street. Right in front of me. Damn! I come into work, shakin' in my shoes, and told Alana here about it. She say it musta been one a them falcons. I was damn glad to hear it. Thought it was a messenger, bringin' me a warnin' 'bout my sinful life!" He polished the counter, making large circles in the wood.

"Don't seem to me that the spirit-keeper would have a sinful life. You look like a good man to me." Elijah squinted at Archibald. "Yeah, you look like a good man to me. That falcon was tellin' you so. It ain't everybody gets to see one. A shy bunch, those falcons. They don't mix with the rest of us."

"Aw, I don't know 'bout that," Archibald said, making larger circles with his cloth.

"Well, I do. And I says he is a good man," Alana spoke up. "He always got a drink waitin' on me when I too cold or too tired to work no more. He let me stay here, when I just *can't* go out anymore. When I had my little girl, Archibald watch her when I gotta go out and hit the streets. Archibald a good man . . . but my baby die."

"Aw, Alana. I didn't do nothin'. I didn't do half the things I shoulda to keep you and the baby safe."

Alana waved away his protest. "You a good man. You just don't like anybody sayin' so."

Elijah touched Alana's hand. "I lost two of my babies. Only they was grown boys and they moved away. I never saw them till they came home dead. I grieve for you, Alana."

Alana's hand shook. She moved her fingers up to her eyes, surprised at the tears dropping onto the counter. "She were only a year old. She got some kinda sickness. I took her to the doctor, but he say she be alright. Just give her some aspirin. I give it to her, but the sickness don't go away. She just get worse! She die one night, in my arms. I was rockin' her and singin' to her, and she just go, like that. It were a long time ago, but it seem like it happen just last night. I'm rockin' and singin' and she die. She die. I never had me no more kids. What for? They die too." She got up and went to the jukebox. She stood there, her face hard-edged in the colored lights.

Archibald looked at Elijah. "She don't talk much about that. Hell, what's to talk about? One years old. One years old! Them doctors oughta be shot, that's what I got to say about it." He turned his back on Elijah and started to polish the glasses.

Elijah walked over to Alana and touched her face. "When they brought my boys' bodies back home, I thought I'd go crazy with all the hurt inside me. Edie never said a word. She just kissed them, then she went outside and walked. She was gone for hours. I was afraid, thought I was goin' to lose her too. But she came back. She was walkin', she said, and found a bird nest that had fallen from a tree. She climbed the tree to put the nest up in the branches. See, there was two little chicks in that nest. Ugly little things, Edie said. No feathers, just those bare little bodies and big hungry beaks. After puttin' the nest back, Edie hid and waited for the mother. She was scared the mother wouldn't come back, or if she did, she wouldn't go near 'cause Edie had touched the nest. Well, she waited and waited, and the mother came back with a mouth full of worms and fed those babies. Then Edie walked home. She said she felt bet- ter 'cause at least somewhere, there was babies that were O.K. My Edie, she was somethin'. When I saw her walkin' toward the house, my heart felt like bustin'. Just the sight of her made me think I could handle all that hurt inside me. My baby boys. They were twins, too. Never did a thing without the other one. I guess maybe it was a good thing they died together. That's what Edie said. One couldn't live without the other. I blamed myself too. Shoulda done this, shoulda done that. Just like you, Alana. But I bet you was a good mother. I can see it."

Alana lifted her head, the lights from the jukebox making pat- terns on her face. "I loved her, you know? She was a little angel in my life. Like a light, you know? I wish I knew that Edie. You must miss her somethin' fierce." They walked back to the counter and sat down. Archibald still had his back to them but was watching them in the mirror.

"I miss her, yes. I miss my boys. But they're still here," he pointed to his chest. "Somewhere here. And I see Edie every once in a while. She keeps an eye on me. I hear her too. She calls, *Elijah, Elijah.* That sweet voice callin'."

"I know! My Cherry Marie, she call me too! She were learnin' to talk and she say, *Mama, Mama,* all the time. I laugh at her. "Don't you know no other words?" I say to her. *Mama, Mama.* I hear that voice, my Cherry Marie callin' me. *Mama.* I hear her and I just want to follow that little voice. *Mama."*

"Don't you be followin' no voices, you hear?" Archibald whirled around and slapped his hand on the wooden surface. "You don't be followin' no voices what call you. You gotta stay here. You alive, woman, and she dead. You can't be followin' no voices." Archibald's eyes were red-rimmed and angry. "Aw, Alana, Alana." He put out his hand and touched her face. His voice became soft, "Don't fol- low no voices. Please, Alana."

Alana brought her hand up to Archibald's. "I won't be followin' her. I just like to hear that voice. Cherry Marie, my baby girl."

Elijah looked away from the two people. Talking about Edie, Cherry Marie, and his baby boys made him lonely, made him long for the sweet faces of the twin girls he loved so much. He felt a hand on his shoulder.

"Don't be feelin' bad, Elijah," Alana said.

"Oh, I ain't feelin' bad, just a little lonesome for my twins. But you know, it's good to talk about death. It's funny, we treat life like it ain't no big deal when it's the biggest deal there is. And we get scared to talk about death. It's just the everyday, death is. Here, have another piece of bread. When you bite into somethin' like this, you know how good life is." He handed a piece to Alana and took one for himself.

Alana took tiny bites of her bread and said, "Them twins be takin' a long time gettin' here. You need a place to stay? I got a place. It clean and warm. Shame on them girls! This here town's not a safe one. Them girls shouldn't be lettin' their grandpa be wanderin' the streets. God knows what could happen!"

"It seems pretty safe to me," Elijah smiled.

Archibald chuckled, "Well, you lucky this time."

"I think I'm pretty lucky. Meetin' you two spirits, I'd say I was a lucky man."

Feeling around in his pockets for change, Elijah announced that he'd call the twins' number again. He went to the phone booth and began dialing.

The door opened and Terrance walked in, ushering Alice and Annie into the bar.

"Grandfather!" the twins shouted and ran to hug him. "There was a terrible accident on the freeway," Alice began.

"No, no, not us," Annie reassured her grandfather.

"We didn't know what to do."

"We were so worried you'd be sitting in that bus station all alone."

"I can't tell you the thoughts that were going through . . ."

"My head," Annie finished.

"You tell the story, Terrance," Alice said, holding on to her grandfather and squeezing his arm.

"Well, I finished my business and went back inside the station, just like I told you I would. I'm standin' there and in walks twins, lookin' worried. I goes up to them and says, you lookin' for Elijah? They don't wanna say, not that I blames them! I told them you was across the street, waitin' on them. But they was nervous like. Can't blame them! But I finally told them what you looks like, that we play Pacman, and you give me a piece of bread. They looked at me like I was crazy, man! Pacman? Grandfather? they say. But it were the bread what did it. They say nobody givin' away bread but Grandfather. Must be him! So they follows me over here to Al's Bar, and here we is."

Alice and Annie laughed, and Annie poked Terrance in the ribs. "Pacman! Grandpa, when did you learn to play Pacman?"

"Today."

For some reason that made the twins laugh even harder.

"Here girls, I want you to meet my friends. Alana. Archibald. We've had a good time here."

Alice and Annie shook hands with Archibald. "Pleased to meet you ladies." Their eyebrows raised only slightly at the sight of Alana while shaking her hand.

Alana said, "So these the famous twins we been hearin' 'bout all night. They're very pretty, Elijah. You must be one proud granddaddy. Girls, your granddaddy's the nicest man. But I 'spect you know that already. I'm very pleased to meet you. Such beautiful hair," and she pointed to the twins' black, shining locks.

"Thank you," said Alice. "Uh . . . I . . ."

"Think you have lovely hair too," Annie finished.

"Oh, girls, it just a wig!" Alana touched the blonde curls and looked pleased.

Archibald lay down his polishing cloth. "What'll it be ladies? Drinks on me. Anybody know 'Lijah, they welcome here anytime."

Alice and Annie looked at each other, looked at their grandfather, looked at each other again, and laughed. "We'll have a beer."

Terrance went to the jukebox and turned on the music. Koko Taylor's pounding voice came blasting out. Terrance snapped his fingers and started singing along.

"Girls, I had a dream on the bus. You were holdin' babies in your arms. They were twins, just like you."

"Oh Grandpa, we don't have any babies. At least not yet. Annie has applied, but we don't know yet."

"Well, that's why I came here. I thought I could help in gettin' you those babies. These Natives down here, they'd listen to an old man like me, now wouldn't they? I dreamed about twin babies, and I'm here to find them for you."

The twins choked a little on their drinks but smiled at their grandfather. "We'll see, Grandpa."

"Yes, we will. Now, I brought whitefish from the Bay. Hope it's still frozen. Your mother made you this fry bread. Alana calls it fry cakes. You liked it, didn't you Alana?"

Alana nodded her agreement. "Just like my grandmama used to make."

Elijah opened the sack. "There's plenty here. Just help yourself."

Terrance was the first one to dip into the bag. "Man, I been dreamin' 'bout this here fry bread since this afternoon. This is good bread!" He chewed ecstatically.

Even Archibald helped himself to a piece. "This *is* like fry cake. I'll be. You tell your mom she make good bread," he told the twins.

They assured him they would relay the message. They hugged their grandfather. "We're so glad you're here. Safe and sound."

"Why wouldn't I be?"

Elijah was very happy. Sharing food was the best thing people could do together. He was anxious to start on this adoption business, but for now, he was content to be with his friends and his twins, eating, laughing.

Outside the sign blinked off, then on. FOOD & SPIRITS. FOOD & SPIRITS. Inside there were music, stories, good food, and friends. Elijah was content.

# A Death In The Family

*for my Uncle*

In 1945, the day Margaret Hill turned nine years old, her mother was murdered. A hit and run, the constable called it. Lily was crossing the street in town when a car closed in on her, running over her, then running out of town. Hit and run.

The white men in uniforms brought her mother's body to the house she shared with Uncle Douglas and Delilah, her grandmother. Limbs twisted and broken, face covered in blood, Lily was unrecognizable from the mother Margaret had loved with all the passion a nine-year-old could feel.

Uncle sobbed and raged over the body of his younger sister. He told the men in uniform he'd kill the driver of the car if he ever found him. The men looked embarrassed and uneasy, anxious to get away from the display of emotion coming from Uncle, like hot wires that snaked and danced in the aftermath of a storm.

"Take it easy, Doug," the constable placated. "It won't do any good to get all riled up."

Uncle slumped on the chair, screams bouncing in his head as he wondered where on this earth an Indian could get justice. The answer was an echo: nowhere, nowhere.

Delilah was silent. Pointing to the kitchen table, her finger instructing the men to lay the body of her daughter on the wooden planks, she was silent. The men left the house, casting glances back at Uncle. Delilah went to her daughter, taking off Lily's shoes, the sturdy brown shoes found in the mission box at church, and stroked her daughter's feet.

Margaret had watched the procession and could not believe this was real. She felt like she did when she was dreaming—outside the events that were happening, not believing this was her mother, her beautiful mother who carefully rolled her hair into a pompadour every day and wore bright dresses and jewelry, who painted her fingernails and toenails with red polish, who applied lipstick with a brush, who was alive, so alive just yesterday. Just yesterday, Lily had promised a special surprise for Margaret's ninth birthday. Just yesterday, Lily had sat with Margaret on her lap and taught her a new song about sitting under an apple tree. Just yesterday, Margaret's world was small and contained within the circle of Mother, Grandmother, and Uncle. Now she saw a huge hole, grabbing at her, waiting to pull her in.

"Mama?"

Uncle looked up at Margaret. He held out his arms to her and she went to him, but her tears were stuck somewhere inside, and she could only let Uncle hold her while she waited for the choking feeling to subside.

Delilah stood up from the kitchen table, still touching her daughter's feet. "You'll help me get your mother ready," she told Margaret. "We'll need to get the others."

"Jesus Christ, let the girl be!" Uncle cried. "She's just a kid."

"Don't take the Lord's name in vain," Delilah said absently, "she'll need to help. Go get the others."

But the others had already heard the death news and were now making their way into the small house, bringing their presence and other gifts for Lily: a piece of braided sweetgrass, a pouch of tobacco, a bottle of whiskey to pass around. The men sat with Uncle, unscrewing the cap to the bottle, talking in low voices. The women ringed themselves around the kitchen table, touching Lily, touching Delilah, trying to hug Margaret, who stood like stone.

"Child, bring us some water."

Margaret went outside and pumped water into the bucket. She carried the heavy burden back to the kitchen, almost stumbling up the steps. On the kitchen table lay her mother, stripped of the bloody rag that used to be her favorite dress. The women had straightened Lily's legs, the legs that were broken and hung at odd angles from her torso. Her mother's body lay, a grotesque imitation of Lily. Margaret brought the bucket of water to the women, who dipped cloths into it and began to wash Lily. The water soon turned red, and Margaret was sent out to get clean. As she dumped the water on the ground, she thought of the water as her mother, her life seeping into the hard ground, making little rivers trickling off into the weeds. A Lily River, Margaret thought. A river of Lily. Margaret pumped the water, her brown braids swinging back and forth. She looked up at the sky, at the cold, dark clouds hovering above the house. She pumped and sang, "Don't sit under the apple tree with anyone else but me," her thin girl voice matching the rhythm of the pump.

Inside the house, Margaret brought the water to the women, who dipped and washed, who applied salve that smelled like mint, who worked silently. Margaret stood off to the side, once again feeling like she was in a dream. She had seen her mother naked lots of times, but never like this—her breasts small and flat, covered with scratches and bruises. Her pubic hair, matted and blood-soaked. Lily's delicate hands were curved into hooklike claws, the red polish on her nails chipped and peeling. This wasn't her mother, Margaret thought. This wasn't her mother.

Margaret looked at the men sitting around the woodstove. They were quiet except for an occasional shout of anger from Uncle. He paced the tiny room, his slick, black hair falling loose from where he had tucked it behind his large ears. Uncle's face was frightening to Margaret. She had always seen him laughing or telling funny stories, his face screwing into shapes that would make her smile. Today his face was that of a stranger, angry, bitter, lips pulled back into a snarl over his gums.

Was it only yesterday, Margaret thought, that Uncle held her hand as they trudged to the Methodist church for Sunday service? He had grumbled, as he always did on Sundays, because Delilah insisted they all go to church. Lily and Delilah walked on ahead, and Uncle held her hand and complained about the minister ("Can't tell a decent story if his life depended on it.") and the hymns ("Why do they have to sing every damn verse of those songs?") and the pacing ("They sing like a funeral march! If they could just speed things up a bit, I wouldn't mind so much."). "Margaret," he'd finished, "your grandmother is a hard woman, to make us do this every damn Sunday of every damn week!" And in church when they started on verse five of "Old Rugged Cross," Uncle had looked at Margaret and whispered, "You'd think the man would finally be dead by now after four verses." She had giggled and hid her face in the hymnal when Delilah gave her a sharp look. Lily had smiled at her brother and winked at Margaret and went on singing verse five in her clear, strong voice.

Was it only yesterday they had walked home and eaten their dinner of potatoes and beans? Uncle and Lily drinking tea by the quart, reusing the leaves and boiling the last bit of flavor from them. Delilah sitting by the stove, mending some piece of clothing and asking Margaret to read from the Bible. Margaret had read a story about a Samaritan helping somebody who lay in the road because nobody else would stop and give aid. She didn't know what a Samaritan was but she was happy reading out loud. Margaret loved to read. She dreamed of someday owning books and being able to pick one up at any time and read to her heart's content. The only book they had in the house was Grandmother's Bible, and Margaret poured over this volume every day.

"That was a good story," Uncle remarked after Margaret had finished.

"It was more than a good story," Delilah said, "it was a lesson. We should always stop to help people who are in need. There are rewards for helping others."

"I guess that's why there ain't any Samaritans around here. They know we can't give out any rewards," Uncle snickered into his hand.

Lily laughed. "If you see any Samaritan, grab 'em quick, before he changes his mind!"

Delilah sighed. "Read another story, Margaret. The one about Joseph's coat of colors."

Margaret looked back at the kitchen table. Delilah was beckoning to her. "Come. Come wash your mother's face. We'll make her pretty again. You'll see. Come."

Margaret took the cloth and went to where her mother's head rested at the head of the table. The women were massaging the mint-scented salve on Lily's arms and legs. They had straightened her crooked fingers and her hands lay at her sides, shining with grease. As Margaret brought the cloth to her mother's face, the sobs that were waiting in her chest came rushing out. Tears from her eyes spilled on Lily's face, mingling with the water on the cloth. The women crooned and continued to rub grease on Lily's breasts, her abdomen, under her arms where the black hairs curled and shone from the salve. Delilah touched Margaret's head. "That's right. See, her face is getting pretty again, just like I said. You're doing a good job. Your mother is pleased you're making her pretty again."

As Margaret washed her mother's face, she could see Lily's features becoming visible. Aside from a long scratch on her right cheek, her face was lovely as ever, almost like she was sleeping, Margaret thought. She tenderly cleaned Lily's forehead, pushing back the black hair. She touched her mother's eyelids, the dark lashes brushing against her fingers. Delilah had a brush in her hand and began untangling Lily's hair and brushing it smooth as it hung over the edge of the table.

"I'll fix her hair, Grandma. I watched her do it. I know how."

Margaret took the brush and drew it through her mother's hair. Rolling puffs on either side of Lily's head and securing them with the hairpins Delilah held in her hand, Margaret worked to get it just right, just the way Lily would have done it. She lifted her mother's head to attach the black snood that held the rest of Lily's long, glossy hair. One of the women held out the jar of grease to her and Margaret lightly smeared it on Lily's face, caressing her mother's features, her nose, her lips.

"She needs her lipstick, Grandma. The red kind."

Delilah brought it to her, and Margaret outlined Lily's full lips, struggling to keep within the lines of her mother's mouth. The women had stopped their work and were watching Margaret leaning over her mother's face, applying the red color to the lifeless mouth. Delilah reached to Margaret, "That's good child. It looks fine."

"No. It has to be just right." She painted the lips, making quick, small strokes like she'd seen Lily do, using her little finger to spread the bright red color. "There." She pulled away from the table and studied her work. "There."

"She looks real pretty, Margaret. You did a good job." Delilah took hold of Margaret's hand, but Margaret pulled away.

"We have to get her dress. The one with the red-and-black squiggles. She liked that one." Margaret walked swiftly to the bureau and began pulling out drawers. Gathering her mother's underpants, slip, and dress, she walked back to the kitchen.

Uncle lurched in front of her, taking hold of her shoulders. "Margaret. My little Margaret. We'll find the one who did this. I'll kill him for sure. We'll find him!" Uncle's face was contorted with grief and anger, the tears pouring out of his eyes. "Your mother, she was the best. Even if she went around with whitemen and pretended she wasn't Indian, she was still the best." His voice slurred by pain and alcohol, Uncle took his hands from Margaret's shoulders and raised a fist into the air. "I'll get him. I'll get him."

"Douglas! That's enough." Delilah's commanding voice sliced the air.

Margaret took her mother's things into the kitchen and handed them to Delilah. The women rolled Lily's body over, pulling on the underpants, the slip. Delilah tore the dress with the red-and-black squiggles and fit it around Lily's body, slipping her arms into the dress and tucking the rest underneath her. Lily was almost ready. Opening Lily's mouth, Delilah inserted the small piece of braided sweetgrass and closed her mouth, sealing the red lips together.

The women gathered their jars, and cloths, and men and left the house, murmuring their condolences and promises to come and sit with Delilah. The house was silent.

Uncle sat by the stove, still staring into the coals. "Mother?" Delilah went to him and took him in her arms. He cried, "She was the best, my sister." Margaret looked at Lily on the kitchen table. She pulled out a chair and sat beside her mother. After a while, Uncle and Delilah came and sat next to her. They waited for the day to come.

In the morning, Margaret woke to find herself in Delilah's arms, a blanket covering them both. Uncle was making tea, his body stooped over like an old man's instead of the thirty-five-year-old he was. Margaret looked over Delilah's shoulder to see if Lily was still there, if maybe it had been a dream after all. But there she lay, stiff and unmoving, her red lips and black hair splayed against the oak table. Delilah stirred and opened her eyes. "Well, it's morning. Got to start cooking. People will be coming." Margaret got off her grandma's lap and stumbled into the bed she had shared with her mother. She lay down and went back to sleep. She didn't dream. The nightmare on the table was enough to last her lifetime.

She woke to the sound of the minister's voice. "I'm so sorry, Delilah."

Uncle lifted the curtain around the bed and sat down beside her. He whispered, "Had to get away. Can't stand the voice of that man." He lit up a cigarette. Margaret could hear the voice of Delilah and that of the Methodist, but couldn't make out the words. "We'll just wait 'til he's gone," Uncle said between puffs of smoke. They soon heard the door being closed and Delilah's, "Douglas? I need some help here." Uncle grinned and put out his cigarette, saving the butt in his pocket. "Got to chop some wood. Wanna help?" Margaret shook her head no. He put out his hand and touched her hair. "Keep going, kid. It's the only way."

Margaret smoothed the bed and went into the kitchen, avoiding the body on the table. Her grandmother was stirring the corn soup in a large kettle. She smiled at Margaret. "It'll be better today. Every day gets a little better. Your mother was just like you when she was little. Serious about everything. She was a good girl, like you."

"What did Uncle mean about Mama pretending not to be an Indian?"

"He didn't mean anything! Just the liquor talking. Your uncle likes his drink too much."

"How much is too much?" Uncle asked, as he hauled wood into the kitchen.

"Never you mind. Just don't upset the child." Delilah continued stirring the soup.

"He doesn't upset me, Grandma." Margaret went to Lily's body and touched her mother's hair.

"Enos will be bringing the coffin soon. Reverend Jameson will be doing the service. You go and get yourself ready. I'll do your hair." Delilah dampened the coals under the kettle.

Margaret opened the bureau drawer and got out her good skirt and sweater: the grey-pleated skirt with suspenders that buttoned in the back and her grey sweater that Delilah had knit from a cast-off found in the mission box. She had unraveled the wool from the man's sweater and rolled it into a ball. With her knitting needles she had made Margaret an almost-new sweater. Margaret got dressed. Delilah came to brush her hair and plait the braids that hung down Margaret's back.

"I used to do this for your mother. Only her hair was coal-black and yours is brown, like the sparrow's wings."

"Why do I have brown hair and not black like Mama's?"

Delilah stopped braiding. "That's because your father didn't have black hair. You must take after him."

"Who was he?"

"Why are you asking that now? Didn't your mother explain all that to you?"

"She just said he died in the war. She didn't tell me he had brown hair. Why wasn't his hair black too?"

Delilah resumed braiding. "Because he was a whiteman."

"Is that what Uncle meant when he said that Mama went around with whitemen?"

"Your mother. . .your mother is dead. I'll have no disrespect in this house toward your mother."

Margaret was silent, her head bursting with questions she couldn't ask. She knew that tone of voice from her grandmother. It meant she had to keep her mouth shut and not ask anything more.

They heard the door open, and Delilah hurried out to greet Enos and the other men bringing the pine box to lay her daughter in. Delilah lined the box with an old quilt. The men lifted Lily's body into the box.

"Wait!" Margaret ran to the box, holding a red satin pillow trimmed in gold fringe. *Niagara Falls* was embroidered on the top in blue silk.

A souvenir, Lily had called it. "A souvenir of my big trip to the Falls. But the best souvenir I got was you," and Lily had hugged Margaret.

Margaret got on her knees and placed the pillow under Lily's head. "There. You can take her now."

Uncle smiled his lopsided grin. "You done good, kid. She'd like that pillow under her head. She sure looks pretty, don't she?" He turned to Delilah. "You go on ahead, Mother. Me and Margaret, we'll follow."

Delilah hurried out the door to catch up to the men carrying the pine box.

Uncle reached into his pants pocket and pulled out a small package wrapped in tissue. "This is your birthday present from your mom. Thought you might want it today. She looked all around for this. Wanted to give you something special for being nine years old. Lily said there was something about being nine. Like it was the beginning of some kind of special thing. I guess for you it is."

Margaret unwrapped the tissue, and in the middle of the paper was a small locket on a chain. "It's beautiful. It's a locket like I saw in a movie. See, you open it up and you can put pictures inside." She opened the tiny hinge and found Lily's face smiling at her. Margaret started to cry huge, gulping sobs that shook her whole body.

Uncle hugged her, his own tears wetting the top of her head. "She was the best, wasn't she? Let me put it around your neck. God, it looks real pretty on you, Margaret. You're gonna be a looker like she was."

"Grandma said my father was a whiteman. Does that mean I'm not an Indian any more?"

"Where'd you get an idea like that? Jesus Christ! Your grandmother is a case for the books. You're a little half-breed, kid. Real special. Lily thought so. I think so. And your grandmother thinks so too. She's just a hard woman sometimes. Goes to church too much. But hell, guess there ain't much else to do in this place. Your grandmother is disappointed in her son. That's me. It rubs off into odd places, but she's a good woman, and you're a good girl."

"Why would Grandma be disappointed in you, Uncle?"

"Aw, kid, I'm not much. Drink too much, fool around too much. I'm thirty-five, kid. Not going anywhere." Uncle's face twisted, and he ran his hand through his hair.

"You're the best uncle in the world," Margaret cried as she hugged the man to her.

"Aw, kid, I'd do anything for you, you know that? Lily always said you were the best thing that ever happened to her. All I know is you're the best thing that happened to me, my little half-breed. You're gonna grow up special. I can feel it. You can read and write. You're real smart, Margaret. That's a gift. I'm real proud of you. So was Lily. She used to tell me that all the time. God, I'm gonna miss her! But we got a piece of her right here. You. And you got a piece of her, right there in that locket. Ain't we lucky?"

Margaret stared down at her locket. "I'm still an Indian?"

"Hell, yes! Anybody says different, you let me know. I'll straighten 'em out." Uncle laughed and pulled her braids. "We better get going. We'll see her out real good, Margaret. We'll see your mother out real good!"

He took her hand and they walked down the road, Margaret's

locket bouncing against her sweater.

The funeral was too long. Reverend Jameson, wanting to give comfort to these people he would never understand, not in a million years, talked, preached, tried to get through to the faces that studied him so politely. To his dismay, the old people came and chanted over the coffin, the women's wrinkled skin and clear eyes daring him to say a word—which he didn't. They sang their songs, spoke prayers in Mohawk, and everyone took a last look at the woman who lay in the pine box. Margaret adjusted the satin pillow and tucked in the few hairs that had come loose from the pompadour that rose so majestically from her mother's head. Delilah kissed her daughter, Uncle took his sister's hand and kissed it. The coffin was nailed shut. They carried the pine box into the cemetery behind the church and lowered it into the hole dug for such a purpose. The people began a song, Uncle's voice rising above the others. They sang Lily into the earth, into another place where she would be in peace. Margaret stood, surrounded by her people, Uncle and Delilah holding her hands, the strong grips keeping her safe. She felt the cold in the air, the coming of winter. She whispered good-bye to her mother.

Back home, the women were busy creating food. The men stood by the woodstove, passing a bottle from mouth to mouth. Some went outside to smoke and tell stories. They brought forth memories of Lily they had been saving for this moment. Old Joseph recalled the time he had taught Lily to step dance. She was his best pupil and had won all contests at the fair thereafter. Uncle told the story of how Lily had been sent to the field by Delilah to pull weeds. She had been five years old and had heard music coming from the ground. She had started to dance and in the process of dancing had not only trampled the weeds, but Delilah's burgeoning potato bean crop. All was forgiven when the girl had carefully replanted each small, green plant—including the weeds! It was true, they all agreed, Lily was one of a kind, the best.

Margaret wandered through the groups of men, the children playing outside. The noise and confusion was soothing to her as she wondered what her life was going to be like without Lily. She wiped her tears with the edge of her sleeve and touched her locket. She thought about growing up, what it meant. What it meant to be an Indian. It might mean that people hated you for reasons known only to them. It might mean that people could run you over with a car and nobody would care. It might mean that Lily died because she was an Indian, even though, as Uncle said, she pretended not to be one. Through her fog of grief she was beginning to feel her history and wonder about herself. A half-breed.

The food was ready. Delilah called to Margaret. She went inside the house and there, on the kitchen table where her mother had laid, were plates and platters of food. Like some miracle in the stories Margaret read aloud, the place of death was transformed into the place of life. Food. Scalloped potatoes resting in milk, pools of oleo making indentations in the oval slices. Two kinds of jello molds—this treat usually reserved for Christmas. Orange jello, blended with carrots and black walnuts picked from Ida's tree. Red jello, stuffed with ground cherries. Each imposing mold sat on a prized plate, a special piece of china. In the kettle, Delilah's corn soup, thick and rich with rabbit meat, white beans, turnips, and lyed corn. The soup was choking with hominy, the broth so thick, the men joked about using forks and knives instead of spoons. There were green beans and wax beans, squash baked with maple syrup. There were onions, creamed whole with salt and a touch of the precious sugar to keep them sweet. Plates and plates of fried bread, grease draining and soaking onto coarse white cloth. Hunks of dough, fried in lard, the outside crisp and brown, the inside heavy and doughy. Dishes of pickled beets and corn relish sat here and there on the table.

The food was ready.

Delilah said grace. "Our heavenly Father, bless this food we are about to receive. In Jesus' name we ask it. Amen."

An old woman spoke in Mohawk, thanking the Creator for giving this food, for giving this day, for giving Lily a chance to walk with her ancestors.

The people each took a plate, holding it to their stomachs like a shield or a gift. Food—always received with gratitude and appetite—especially at death, the women's miracle turning the kitchen table to sustenance and life. Food. The plenty of the table on this day staving off hunger of another kind. Gifts filling stomachs and souls.

Uncle took Margaret's hand and talked about his obligation to Lily's memory and to her daughter. Tears ran down his twisted nose as he recited the words.

Delilah took Margaret's other hand and said, "Of all the gifts that came from Lily, this is the greatest of them all. Let us eat."

Margaret held her plate and touched her locket. She closed her eyes and the face of Lily smiled, then disappeared.

The people filled their plates and began to eat.

# Turtle Gal

Sue Linn's mama was an Indian. She never knew from where, only that Dolores wore a beaded bracelet: yellow, blue, and green beads woven into signs. Burnt out from alcohol and welfare, Dolores gave up late one afternoon, spoke to her daughter in an unknown language, and put the bracelet around her girl's skinny wrist where it flopped over her hand. She turned her face to the wall and died. November 4, 1968.

Sue Linn watched her mother die, knowing by instinct that it was better this way. Better for Dolores. But her child mind, her nine-year-old mind, had not yet thought of the possibilities or penalties that lay in wait for little girls with no mother. She thought of her friend, James William Newton, who lived across the hall. She went and got him. He walked Sue Linn back to the room where her mother lay dead.

"Lord, lord, lord, lord," the old man chanted as he paid his respects, covering the still-warm woman with the faded red spread. His tired eyes, weeping, looked down at the child standing so close to him. "Go get your things now, little gal. Bring everything you got. Your clothes, everything."

With his help, Sue Linn removed all traces of herself from the darkening apartment. James William made a last, quick search, then told the child to say good-bye to her mama. He waited in the hall,

My thanks to Tom King for the title suggestion.

his face wrinkled and yellowish. His hand trembled as he reached into his pants pocket for his handkerchief, neatly folded. He shook the thin, white cloth and brought it to his eyes where he wiped the cry, then blew his nose.

Sue Linn stood beside the bed she and her mother had shared for as long as the girl could remember. She pulled the spread from her mother's face and looked intensely at Dolores. Dolores' face was quieter, younger looking. Her broad nose seemed somehow more delicate, and her dark lashes were like ink marks against her smooth, reddish cheek. Sue Linn felt a choking move from her stomach up through her heart, her lungs, her throat and mouth. With an intake of harsh breath, she took a lock of her mother's black hair in her small fist. She held on, squeezing hard, as if to pull some last piece of life from her mother. She let go, turned away, and closed the door behind her. James William was waiting, his arms ready to hold her, to protect her.

Together, they opened his door, walked into the room that was welcoming and waiting for their presence. African violets sat in a row along the windowsill, their purple and blue flowers shaking from the force of the door being closed. Sue Linn went to touch the fuzzy heart leaves, wondering once again what magic the old man carried in him to grow these queer, exotic plants in the middle of a tired, dirty street.

James William put aside the bag filled with Sue Linn's belongings and told the child to sit in his chair while he went to call the ambulance. "Don't answer the door. Don't make no sounds. Sit quiet, little gal, and I be's back in a wink." He hugged the child and went out the door.

Sue Linn sat on James William's favorite chair, a gold brocade throne with arms that curved into high, wide wings. She stared out the window. She looked past the violets, past the ivy hanging in a pot attached to threads, dangling fresh and alive in front of the glass. She looked onto the street, the avenue that held similar apartment buildings, large and grey. Some had windows knocked out, some had windows made bright by plastic flowers. Some had windows decorated with a cross and Jesus Is My Rock painted on from the inside. The Salvation Army complex stood low and squat, the lights beginning to be turned on, bringing a softening sheen to the beige cement. The air was cold, the people on the street pulling their coats and jackets closer to their bodies as they walked, hunched over in struggle past the Chinese restaurants, the grocery, the bars, the apartments. Cars made noise—the noises of rust, of exhaust pipes ready to fall off, of horns applied with angry hands. Buses were unloading people, doors opening to expel faces and bodies of many shapes and colors. The avenue seemed to wander forever in a road of cement, tall buildings, people, machines, eventually stopping downtown, caught up in another tangle of streets and boulevards.

James William walked down the three flights of stairs to the pay-phone in the lobby. He called the operator to report the dead woman, walked back up the three flights of stairs, his thoughts jumping and beating against his brain as his heart lurched and skipped from the climb. When he entered his room the child turned to look at him. "They be here soon, child. Now we not lettin' on you here with me. We be very quiet. We lets them medical peoples take care a things. We don't say one word. Ummhmm, we don't say a word."

He came to the window and watched for the ambulance that eventually came screaming to the curb. Two white men, their faces harried and nervous, got out of the ambulance and entered the building. A police car followed. The cops went into the building where the super was arguing with the medics.

"I don't know nothin' about a dead woman! Who called you? Who did you say she was?"

The officers hurried things along, the super angrily getting out his keys. "If it's 3D, then it's that Indian. She's all the time drinkin' and carryin' on. Her and that sneaky, slant-eyed kid ain't nothin' but trouble. Who did you say called in? Nobody let on to me!"

On the third floor, cops, medics, and super formed a phalanx around the door to 3D. Knocking and getting no answer, they unlocked the door and entered the room. Up and down the hall, doors were opened in cracks. Eyes looked out, gathering information that would be hoarded and thought about, then forgotten.

"Anybody know this woman?" the cops shouted in the hall.

Doors closed. Silence answered. One of the cops pounded on a door. A very old woman opened it, a sliver of light behind her.

"Do you know this woman in 3D? When was the last time you saw her?"

Her dark brown face resettled its lines as she spoke. "I don' know her. She was an Injun lady. One a them Injuns from out west, I guess. I don' know nothin'."

The officer waved his hand in disgust. He and his partner started down the stairs, their heavy black shoes scratching the steps, the leather of their holsters squeaking as they rubbed against the guns.

James William stood, his ear pressed to the door. Sue Linn continued to stare out the window. There were sounds of feet moving away, sounds of hard breathing as the body of Dolores was carried down the three flights of stairs and into the cold November twilight.

James William Newton turned from the door. He was eighty years old. He was a singer of the blues. He was the Prince of Georgia Blues. He was Sweet William. He went to the kitchenette and put the kettle on to boil. He moved slowly to the cupboard, taking out a pot and settling it on the tiny stove. Everything surrounding Sweet William was small and tiny like him. The table, covered in blue oilcloth, was just big enough for two. Little wooden chairs were drawn tight to the edge of the table, waiting for his hands to arrange the seating. The one window in the kitchenette was hung with starched white curtains trimmed in royal blue rickrack. A single wall was papered in teapots and kettles, red and blue splashed on a yellow background. The wall was faded from age but still looked cheerful and surprising. A cupboard painted white held thick dishes and the food. Rice, red beans, spices, cornmeal, salt, honey, and sugar. A cardboard box placed on the cracked yellow linoleum contained potatoes and onions, the papery skins sometimes falling to the floor, coming to rest by the broom and dustpan leaning against the teapot wall.

On the first night of Sue Linn's new life, she watched Sweet William work in the kitchen, her eyes following his round body as he walked the few steps across the linoleum, taking leaves out of a tin box, placing them in a brown pot, pouring the whistling water over the tea. He replaced the lid on the teapot, removed a tea cozy from a hook, and placed this over the pot. The child, ever fascinated by Sweet William's routine, his fussy kitchen work, his hands dusting and straightening, felt comforted by the familiar activity. Often James William made supper for the girl. Cooking up the rice, a towel wrapped around his fat waist, mashing the potatoes, adding canned milk and butter. Sometimes, there was ham hocks or chitlins. The hot, pungent dishes were magic, made from Sweet William's hands and the air and salt.

James William sang quietly as he busied himself with the pot of soup. His eyes grabbed quick looks toward the chair and the thin, golden child who watched him with blank eyes. Little folds of flesh covered her eyelids which rapidly opened and closed. Sitting like that, so still, her eyes blinking, blinking, she reminded the old man of a turtle he'd seen a long time ago, home in Georgia.

Poking around in the marsh, he and his friends had found a spotted turtle upside-down, struggling to put itself right. He had picked up the turtle and looked at its head, pulling in, eyefolds closing over the eyes in panic, opening, closing, staring at him. He had set the turtle on its legs, where it continued on. The boys had laughed at the creature's slow journey. James William remembered the turtle, remembered his friends—the sweetness of them. Memories like this appeared in a haze. When they came to him, he clutched at them, holding onto each moment—afraid he would never see them again. He stood in the kitchenette and recalled the day of the turtle. He called forth the weather, so hot and lush, you could hold the air in your hand and feel it wet on your skin. He called forth the smell of the marsh—a green smell, a salty smell. He recalled the reeds, pulled from the mud and stuck between their lips, the taste of bitter grass mingling with another taste of sweet—like the stick of licorice his daddy had once brought him from town. He tried to call forth his friends, their names, their brown-and-tan colors, but the memory was fading. Yet, he remembered the black skin of Isaac, his best friend of all. Remembered when Isaac held his arm, the thin fingers spread out looking like molasses spilled against his own yellow, almost white-looking arm. Isaac.

"Isaac?"

Stirring the soup, he sang bits of song culled from memories of his mama, church, and memories of the band—Big Bill and the Brown Boys. Tunes spun from his lips. Notes and chords played in his throat, starting somewhere in his mind, trickling down through his scratchy voice box, coming out round, weeping, and full. Sweet William sang, his face shifting as he wove the music in and out of his body. His head moved and dipped. His shoulders jerked and shrugged to emphasize a word, a phrase. To Sue Linn, it was as pleasurable to watch Sweet William sing as it was to listen. His words and music were almost always the same. Words that came from a heartache, a home with no furniture.

"Lord, what I gonna do with this here child? Now listen up, girl. You gonna be my little gal. We be mama and little gal. We be a family. Ummhmm, anybody ask, you be mine. It ain't gonna be easy. Old James William here, he gots to think of some heavy talkin' to fool them peoples what be snoopin' around here. Them government types. Yes ma'am, James William gots to think of some serious talk. Lord! Old man like myself with a child. A baby! I tells you, you know I never be's married. Leastwise, not no marriage like the government peoples thinks is right. Just me and Big Bill, movin' with that band. Me bein' a fool many a time over some sweet boy what talks with a lotta sugar but don' make no sense. But that Big Bill, he were some man. Always take me back, like I never did no wrong. Yes ma'am, I be a fool for a pretty boy. But I always got a little work. Workin' on them cars sometime. Child, I swear the metal in my blood! I still hear that noise. Whoo, it like to kill me! That noise, them cars hurryin' along the line, waitin' for a screw here, a jab there. But I worked it. I worked it. Yes I did. And me and Big Bill, we make a home. Yes we did. We did. And before the sugar and the high bloods get him, we make a home. We was a family, that fine man and me.

Ummhmmm.

"Now look at her sit there with them turtle eyes. She can't talk. Now listen here, baby. You mama at rest now, bless her sorry little life. You got you another kinda mama now. I take care my baby. You mama so peaceful now. With angels and the Indians. She make that transition over, ummhmm. She be happy. Now, I gots to make this here turtle gal happy. You gots to cry sometime, child. Honey lamb, you gots to cry! If you don' grieve and wail, it get all caught up in you, start to twist your inside so bad. Girl! It hurt not to cry. You listen to this old man. Sweet William, he know what he talkin' 'bout."

*I sing because I'm happy*
*I sing because I'm free*
*His eye is on the sparrow*
*And I know he watches me.*

The old man began his song in a whisper. As he ladled out the soup into bowls, he switched from hymn to blues, the two fitting together like verse and chorus. He nodded his head toward the child, inviting her to sing with him. Sue Linn's thin voice joined James William's fat one.

*Heaven's cryin,' seem like the rain keep comin' down*
*Heaven's cryin,' seem like the rain keep comin' down*
*That heaven don' let up*
*Since my baby left this mean ole town.*

They sang together. They sang for Dolores. They sang for Big Bill. They sang for each other. Blues about being poor, being colored, being out of pocket. Blues about home—that sweet, hot, green-and-brown place. Home was a place where your mama was, waiting on a porch, or cooking up the greens. Home was where you were somebody. Your name was real, and the people knew your name and called you by that name. It was when you left that home that your name became an invisible thing. You got called new names— *Nigger, Bitch, Whore, Shine, Boy*. It was when you left that home you started to choke on your name and your breath and a new kind of blues was sung.

The old man came from the kitchen and picked the child up

in his arms, set her on his lap in the brocade chair, covered them with his special afghan, and the two rocked and swayed.

"She like a bird, no weight on her at all, at all. I *do* likes a rock in this old chair. It help a person think and study on things what ails us. Yes ma'am, just a rockin' and a studyin' on them things."

Sue Linn's tears began. Soon she sobbed, the wails moving across the room, coming back in an echo. James William sang, crooned, wiped her eyes and his with the dry palms of his hands.

"My baby. My turtle gal. Lord, I remember my own mama's passin'. It hurt so bad. She were a good woman, raisin' us ten kids. My daddy workin' his body to an early grave. It hurt when a mama die. Seem like they should always just go on bein' our mama. You mama, she try her best. She were a sad woman. She love you, little gal. And I loves you. We be a family now. Big Bill! You hears that? A family. Sue Linn Longboat and James William Newton. Now ain't they gonna look twict at this here family? I tell you. I tell *you!* It be alright, my baby girl. It be alright."

Sue Linn stopped crying as suddenly as she had started. Her thin face with the slanted eyes, small nose, and full lips subdued itself. "But Sweet William, I hear people talk about heaven. My mom didn't believe in it, but where will she go now? I don't know where she is. And sometimes. . . sometimes she said she wished I never was born."

The girl stared into the old man's face, trusting him to give her the answers. Trusting him to let her know why she ached so much, why she always felt alone and like a being who didn't belong on this earth. His skin was smooth, except for the cracks around his eyes and down his cheeks, ending at the corners of his mouth. His eyes were brown and yellow and matched the color of his skin, like mottled corn, covered with hundreds of freckles. He had few teeth except for a startlingly white stump here and there. When he opened his mouth to sing, it looked like stars on a black map. His lips were wide and brown. His nose was flat, the nostrils deep.

"Baby, I don' know 'bout no heaven. My mama truly believed it. But I thinks this here story 'bout pearly gates and all is just a trick.

Seem like they ain't nothin' wrong with this here earth. The dirt gonna cover your mama and that be alright with her. She miss the sky and the wind and the land. Told me plenty a times. Seem like, compared to that heaven where the peoples hang playin' harps and talkin' sweet, this here earth ain't so bad. You mama, she be mighty unhappy in a heaven where they ain't no party or good lovin' goin' on. Seem like that heaven talk just a way to gets the peoples satisfied with the misery they has to bear in this here world. Once you gets to thinkin' that a reward waitin' on you for bein' poor and colored, why it just beat you down more. You don' stops to think 'bout doin' somethin' 'bout it right here, right now. Ummhmm, them white peoples, they thinks a everything. But there be a lot they don' know. Everything don' always mean *every thing!* I do believe Dolores more at rest in the brown dirt. And lord, child, from jump every mama wish her children never be born sometime! That's a fact. Ummhmm. Honey, she love you. She just too full a pain to remember to *tell* you.

It just like me and Big Bill. Why, they be days we forgets to say, 'Big Bill, you my onliest one. James William, you sure one fine man.' Then you gets to thinkin', hey, this man don' love me no more! And you gets afraid to ask, 'cause you thinkin' that's *his* duty to remember. Then you gets mad and sad all together and it get all mixed up and then you speakin' in shortness and evil kinda ways. You forgets that everybody be carryin' his own pain and bad things. The disrememberin' be a thing that happen though. We be foolish, us peoples. Ain' no way gettin' 'round that! Seem like, if we be perfect, we be like them white peoples up there in that heaven they thinks so special. Yes, yes, we be in that white heaven, with the white pearly gates, and the white robes, and the white slippers. Child! You ever think 'bout heaven always bein' so white? Lord child! Whooo!"

He laughed and laughed, hugging Sue Linn tight, his chest rumbling in her ear. She laughed too, even though she wasn't sure she knew the joke. But it made her feel better to be sitting in Sweet William's lap, her head pressed to his heart, the afghan of bright colors covering her coldness and fright. She used to laugh with Dolores. Mostly over Dolores' mimicry of the people on the street or in the

bars. She had almost become those people, so good was she at capturing a gesture, a voice, a way of holding her body. There was no
meanness in the foolery; just fun, just a laugh, a present for Sue Linn.

"Now, my turtle gal, this old colored man be talkin' more than
his due. I says, after a song and a good cry, they ain' nothin' better
than hot soup and peppermint tea. I thinks I even gots a little ba-
nana cake saved for you."

They unfolded from the brocade chair and went to the table.
The tiny, round Black man of light skin. The tiny, thin girl of gold
skin and Indian hair, her body wrapped in the afghan crocheted by
Sweet William's hands. As James William poured the tea, his white
shirt dazzled the girl's eyes. She watched his short legs walk slowly
to the stove, his small feet wearing the felt slippers he never seemed
to take off. He was wearing his favorite pants—grey flannel with handsome pleats and small cuffs at the bottom. He was wearing the only
belt Sue Linn had ever seen him wear—a wide alligator strip with
a buckle of solid silver, round and etched with the words *Florida
Everglades*. It had been a gift from Big Bill so many years ago, the
date and reason for the gift were lost in James William's memory.
He only remembered Big Bill's face as he handed the belt to Sweet
William, the pale mocha of his skin flushing and reddening as he
pushed the tissue-wrapped gift toward James William, saying, "Here,
honey. For you. A gift." James William's starched, white shirt had
cuffs that were turned back and fastened with silver-colored links,
a red stone gleaming in the center of each piece of metal. Sue Linn
stared at the stones that seemed to signal on-off-stop. Red means
stop. . . .

She had learned that in school when she started kindergarten.
That was four years ago. She was in third grade now, a big girl. She
liked school. At least, she liked it when she went, when her mom
remembered to send her. When Sue Linn felt safe to ask Dolores
to braid her long hair without making the woman cry. When Dolores
was in a good mood from having extra money and bought Sue Linn
plaid dresses, white socks, and shoes that were shiny and had buckles

instead of laces. She talked loud at these times, talked about how her baby was just as good as anybody, and anyway, she was the prettiest kid in school by far. Sue Linn had a hard time understanding this talk. Everyone in school wore old clothes and shoes with laces. It didn't make sense. Maybe it had to do with the picture magazines that showed up around the apartment. The people on the shiny pages were white and stood in funny poses. They wore fancy clothes and coats made from animals. They looked like they were playing statues, which Sue Linn had played once with the kids at school. It was a scary feeling to stop and stand so still until the boss kid said you could move. She liked it though. It made her feel like she was invisible. If she were really a statue, she'd be made out of wood or stone—something hard.

Sort of like the statues at the place her teacher, Miss Terrell, had taken them. Miss Terrell called the giant building a museum and said the statues were sculptures. She pointed out one made by a Black man. She took them to see a display case that had Indian jewelry resting on pieces of wood, only Miss Terrell called it Native American art. Sue Linn thought of her mother's beaded bracelet and stared at the glass case. It made her want to cry for a reason she couldn't even begin to think about. She remembered the Indian case for a long time after. She told her mom about it, and Dolores said it would be nice to go there; she had gone there once, she thought. But they never talked about it again. No, Sue Linn was not a statue. She was bony and covered with soft, gold skin and black hair that was coarse and reached below her shoulder blades. She practiced statues at home, standing on the worn green couch, trying to see herself in the wavy mirror on the opposite wall.

"Getting stuck on yourself, honey? That's how I started. A grain of salt, honey. That's what we need to take ourselves with. We're just bones and skin, honey. Bones and skin."

The child thought her mother much more than bones, skin, and salt. She thought Dolores was beautiful and was proud to walk with her on the avenue. The day they got the food stamps was one of the best days, for a while. Dolores was sober on those days. She would sit at the card table making lists and menus. Dolores labored hard on those days, looking through her magazines, cutting out recipes for "tasty, nutritional meals within your budget." Sue Linn stayed close to her mother on days like that, fascinated by Dolores' activity.

"How would you like chicken vegetable casserole on Monday? Then on Tuesday we could have Hawaiian chicken. I found a recipe for peanut butter cookies. It says here that peanut butter is a good source of protein. Would you like Dolores to make you cookies, baby? Maybe we could make them together." Sue Linn shook her head yes and stood even closer to her mother. Shiny paper with bright colors of food lay emblazoned on the table. Sue Linn was caught by Dolores' words, her magic talk of casseroles and cookies. Writing down words that came back as food. Food was something real yet mysterious. Food was something there never was enough of. Sue Linn ate a free lunch at school. Always hungry, eating too fast, not remembering what she ate, just eating then being hungry again.

Each morning Miss Terrell asked if anyone had forgotten to eat breakfast, because she just happened to bring orange juice and graham crackers from home. Miss Terrell must be magic because there was always enough for everyone. Miss Terrell was black, almost pure black like the stone set in the school door proclaiming when it was built (1910) and whose name it was built to honor (Jeremy Comstock). Marble, yes, that's what Miss Terrell called it. Black marble, that was Miss Terrell's skin. Her hair was cut close to her head and curled tightly against her scalp. James William's hair was like this, but more bushy, and his hair was white while Miss Terrell's was black with a red cast in the sunlight. She wore red lipstick, sometimes purple to go with the dress with white and pink dots on the sash. Her clothes were beautiful. Blue skirt and red jacket. Green dress with gold buttons. Her shoes were red or black shiny stuff with pointy, pointy toes and little wooden heels. Miss Terrell was tall and big. Some of the boys whispered and laughed about Miss Terrell's "boobs." Sue Linn saw nothing to laugh about, only knowing that boys giggled about sex things. She thought Miss Terrell's chest was very wonderful. It stuck out far and looked proud in a way. When she told this to Sweet William, he said, "Child, that Alveeta Terrell be a regular proud woman. Why wouldn't her chest be as proud as the rest of her? You lucky as can be to have proud Miss Alveeta Terrell be your teacher!"

One time, and it was the best time, Miss Terrell had come to school in a yellow dress over which she wore a length of material made from multicolored threads of green, red, purple, yellow, and black. She called it Kente cloth and told the class it was woven in Africa and the people, even the men, wore it every day. She said she was wearing this special cloth because it was a special day. It was a day that Black people celebrated being African, and even though they might live in all kinds of places, they had come from Africa at one time. Then she showed them a map of Africa and traced lines running from that continent to North America, to the West Indies, to South America, to just about everywhere. Amos asked, if Africa was so special, why did the people leave? Miss Terrell said that the people didn't leave because they wanted to, but because these other people—Spanish, British, American, and French—had wanted slaves to work on their lands and make things grow for them so they could get rich. And these same people killed Indians in North America to get land. And these people had captured Africans as if they were herds of animals. They had put them in chains and shipped them to lands where their labor was needed. Some Africans had died trying to escape, some from hunger, thirst, and disease, but some had stayed alive to reach the new land that was a stranger to them.

The children pondered on these facts before raising their hands to ask questions. Miss Terrell answered in her sure voice. She knew everything. She told them about Denmark Vesey, Nat Turner, John Brown, Chrispus Attucks, whose last name meant *deer* because his mama had been a Choctaw Indian. She told them about Touissant L'Overture, about the Maroons in Jamaica, about Harper's Ferry. She told them about the Seminoles and Africans in Florida creating an army to fight the U.S. soldiers and how they had won the fight! Sue Linn's mind was so filled with these wondrous facts, she dreamed about them that night. And it came to her in the dream that Miss Terrell was a food-giver. Her thoughts and facts were like the graham crackers she laid out on her desk each morning. They were free to take, to eat right at that moment, or to save for when one got really hungry. The next morning, Sue Linn copied down her dream in the little notebook she carried with her everywhere. "Miss Terrell is a food-giver." She told Sweet William, who agreed.

Food stamp day. Dolores making something out of nothing. What did it mean? Everything meant something. This she had learned on her own, from the streets, from being a kid. She wanted to talk with Dolores about this, but was too shy.

Dolores was ready. Sue Linn puttered at the table, stalling for time, prolonging the intimacy with her mother. Sue Linn was not ready for the store. *It* happened every time. Dolores got sad. The store defeated her. It was a battle to see how far down the aisles she could get before giving up. The limp vegetables, the greenish-brown meat, the lack of anything resembling the food in the magazines. Sue Linn sensed it before it happened. The faint shrug of Dolores' shoulders, the shake of her head as if clearing it from a dream. Then they proceeded fast, Dolores grabbing at things that were cheap and filling, if only for a few hours. The little girl tried calling her mother's attention to funny people in the store, or some fancy-packaged box of air and starch. Anything, *please, please,* to get that look off her mother's face. That look of fury and contempt. That look of sadness and loss. They would end up with a few things like bread, canned corn, and maybe, hamburger. All her food stamps gone, they'd put the groceries away and Dolores would go out and not return until the next day with a few dollars and a raging headache.

Dolores picked up her lists and stamps, placed them in her purse, a beige plastic bag with her initials stamped in gold letters: D. L., Dolores Longboat. She went to the wavy mirror and, with her little finger, applied blue eye shadow because "you never know who we'll meet." She brushed her black hair until it crackled with sparks and life across her wide back. Dressed in too-tight jeans, a pink sweater frayed and unraveling at the bottom, her gold-tone earrings swinging and dancing, she defied anyone or anything to say she didn't exist. "Let's go."

Sue Linn took hold of her mother's hand and stared up at Dolores, as if to burn the image of her mama into her brain, as if to keep the scent of lily-of-the-valley cologne in her nose. The brown eyes shaded in blue looked down at her child. Dark eye watched dark eye—two females locked in an embrace of color, blood, and bewildering love. Dolores broke the intensity of the moment, cast her eyes around the apartment, commiting to memory what she had to come home to. Tightening her hold on Sue Linn's hand, she said once again, "Let's go." She set the lock and the two went out into the street.

Sue Linn's eyes closed with this last memory. Her head nodded above the soup. James William rose from the table and pulled the bed down from the wall. Straightening the covers and fluffing the pillow, he made the bed ready for the child's tired body and heart. He picked her up and carried her the few feet to the bed. Taking off her shoes, he gently placed the girl under the blanket and tucked the pillow under her head. He placed the afghan at the foot of the bed, folded and neat.

James William Newton—Sweet William—went to his chair and sat in the nighttime light. He could see a piece of the moon through a crack between two buildings across the street.

"Ole moon, what you think? I gots this here child now. Them government peoples be wantin' to know where this child be. Or is they? Seem like the whereabouts of a little gal ain' gonna concern too many a them. Now, I ain' worryin' 'bout raisin' this here turtle gal. It one a them things I be prepared to do. But Moon, we gots to have a plan. I an old man. This here baby need me. Yes, ma'am. There gots to be some providin' to do. Big Bill? Is you laughin' at me? It be a fix we in. Ummhmm, a regular fix. Big Bill? I needs a little a that talk you always so ready with. Honey, it ever be a wonder to me how a man could talk so much and *still* make sense like you done! I sittin' here waitin' on you, honey. Sweet William, he waitin' on you."

He sat through the night, refilling his cup many times. His memories came and went like the peppermint tea he drank. His lips moved in conversation and song. Sometime before dawn he laughed and murmured, "Thank you, honey. You always was the bestest man." He drank his last cup, rinsed it, and set it upside-down in the sink. He settled his body on the blue davenport, the afghan pulled up to his shoulders. He looked one more time at the sleeping child, her dark hair hiding her face in sleep.

"Child, sleep on and dream. Sweet William, he here. Me and Big Bill take care of our baby, turtle gal. You be alright. Yes, ma'am, you be alright."

He closed his eyes and slept.

# Swimming Upstream

Anna May spent the first night in a motel off Highway 8. She arrived about ten, exhausted from her long drive—through farmland, bright autumn leaves, the glimpse of blue lake. She saw none of this, only the grey highway stretching out before her. She stopped when the motel sign appeared, feeling the need for rest, it didn't matter where.

She took a shower, lay in bed, and fell asleep, the dream beginning again almost immediately. Her son—drowning in the water, his skinny arms flailing the waves, his mouth opening to scream with no sound coming forth. She, Anna May, moving in slow motion into the waves, her hands grabbing for the boy but feeling only water run through her fingers. She grabbed frantically, but nothing held to her hands. She dove and opened her eyes under water and saw nothing. He was gone. Her hands connected with sand, with seaweed, but not her son. He was gone. Simon was gone.

Anna May woke. The dream was not a nightmare anymore. It had become a companion to her, a friend, almost a lover—reaching for her as she slept, making pictures of her son, keeping him alive while recording his death. In the first days after Simon left her, the dream made her wake screaming, sobbing, arms hitting at the air, legs kicking the sheets, becoming tangled in the material. Her bed was a straightjacket, pinning her down, holding her until the dream ended. She would fight the dream then. Now, she welcomed it.

During the day she had other memories of Simon. His birth,

his first pair of shoes, his first steps, his first word—*Mama*—his first book, his first day of school. His firsts were also his lasts, so she invented a future for him during her waking hours: his first skating lessons, his first hockey game, his first reading aloud from a book, his first. . . But she couldn't invent beyond that. His six-year-old face and body wouldn't change in her mind. She couldn't invent what she couldn't imagine.

She hadn't been there when Simon drowned. Simon had been given to her ex-husband by the courts. She was judged unfit. Because she lived with a woman. Because a woman, Catherine, slept beside her. Because she had a history of alcoholism. The history was old. Anna May had stopped drinking when she became pregnant with Simon, and she had stayed dry all those years. She couldn't imagine what alcohol tasted like after Simon was born. He was so lovely, so new. Her desire for a drink evaporated every time Simon took hold of her finger, or nursed from her breast, or opened his mouth in a toothless smile. She had marveled at his being—this gift that had emerged from her own body. This beautiful being who had formed himself inside her, had come with speed through the birth canal to welcome life outside her. His face red with anticipation, his black hair sticking straight up as if electric with hope, his little fists grabbing, his pink mouth finding her nipple and holding on for dear life. She had no need for alcohol. There was Simon.

Simon was taken away from them. But they saw him on weekends, Tony delivering him on a Friday night, Catherine discreetly finding someplace else to be when Tony's car drove up. They still saw Simon, grateful for the two days out of the week they could play with him, they could delight in him, they could pretend with him. They still saw Simon, until the call came that changed all that. The call from Tony saying that Simon had drowned when he fell out of the boat as they were fishing. Tony sobbing, "I'm sorry. I didn't mean for this to happen. I tried to save him. I'm sorry. Please, Anna, please forgive me. Oh God, Anna. I'm sorry. I'm sorry."

So Anna May dreamed of those final moments of a six-year-old life. And it stunned her that she wasn't there to see him die when she had been there to see him come into life.

Anna May stayed dry, but she found herself glancing into cupboards at odd times. Looking for something. Looking for something to drink. She thought of ways to buy wine and hide it so she could take a drink when she needed it. But there was Catherine. Catherine would know, and Catherine's face, already so lined and tired and old, would become more so. Anna May saw her own face in the mirror. Her black hair had streaks of grey and white she hadn't noticed before. Her forehead had deep lines carved into the flesh, and her eyes, her eyes that had cried so many tears, were a faded and washed-out blue. Her mouth was wrinkled, the lips parched and chapped. She and Catherine, aged and ghostlike figures walking through a dead house.

Anna May thought about the bottle of wine. It took on large proportions in her mind. A bottle of wine, just one, that she could drink from and never empty. A bottle of wine, the sweet, red kind that would take away the dryness, the withered insides of her. She went to meetings but never spoke, only saying her name and "I'll pass tonight." Catherine wanted to talk, but Anna May had nothing to say to this woman she loved. She thought about the bottle of wine: the bottle, the red liquid inside, the sweet taste gathering in her mouth, moving down her throat, hitting her bloodstream, warming her inside, killing the deadness.

She arranged time off work and told Catherine she was going away for a few days. She needed to think, to be alone. Catherine watched her face, the framing of the words out of her mouth, her exhausted eyes. Catherine said, "I understand."

"Will you be alright?" Anna May asked her.

"Yes, I'll be fine. I'll see friends. We haven't spent time with them in so long, they are concerned about us. I'll be waiting for you. I love you so much."

Anna May got in the car and drove up 401, up 19, over to 8 and the motel, the shower, the dream.

Anna May smoked her cigarettes and drank coffee until daylight. She made her plans to buy the bottle of wine. After that, she had no plans, other than the first drink and how it would taste and feel.

She found a meeting in Goderich and sat there, ashamed and angered with herself to sit in a meeting and listen to the stories and plan her backslide. She thought of speaking, of talking about Simon, about the bottle of wine, but she knew someone would stop her or say something that would make her stop. Anna May did not want to be stopped. She wanted to drink and drink and drink until it was all over. *My name is Anna May and I'll just pass.*

Later, she hung around for coffee, feeling like an infiltrator, a spy. A woman took hold of her arm and said, "Let's go out and talk. I know what you're planning. Don't do it. Let's talk."

Anna May shrugged off the woman's hand and left. She drove to a liquor outlet. Vins et Spiriteaux. *Don't do it.* She found the wine, one bottle, that was all she'd buy. *Don't do it.* One bottle, that was all. She paid and left the store, the familiar curve of the bottle wrapped in brown paper. *Don't do it.* Only one bottle. It wouldn't hurt. She laughed at the excuses bubbling up in her mouth like wine. Just one. She smoked a cigarette in the parking lot, wondering where to go, where to stop and turn the cap that would release the red, sweet smell before the taste would overpower her and she wouldn't have to wonder anymore.

She drove north on 21, heading for the Bruce Peninsula, Lake Huron on her left, passing the little resort towns, the cottages by the lake. She stopped for a hamburger and, without thinking, got her thermos filled with coffee. This made her laugh, the bottle sitting next to her, almost a living thing. She drank the coffee driving north, with her father—not Simon, not Catherine—drifting in her thoughts. Charles, her mother had called him. Everyone else called him Charley. Good old Charley. Good-time Charley. Injun Charley. Charles was a hard worker, working at almost anything. He worked hard, he drank hard. He tried to be a father, a husband, but the work and the drink turned his attempts to nothing. Anna May's mother never complained, never left him. She cooked and kept house and raised the children and always called him Charles. When Anna May grew up, she taunted her mother with the fact that *her Charles* was a drunk. Why didn't she care more about her kids than her drunken husband? Didn't her mother know how ashamed they were to have such a father, to hear people talk about him, to laugh at him, to laugh at them—the half-breeds of good-old-good-time-Injun Charlie?

Anna May laughed again, the sound ugly inside the car. Her father was long dead and, she supposed, forgiven by her. He had been a handsome man back then, her mother a skinny, pale girl, an orphan girl, something unheard of by her father. How that must have appealed to the romantic that he was. Anna May didn't know how her mother felt about the life she'd had with Charles. Her mother never talked about those things. Her mother, who sobbed and moaned at Simon's death as she never had at her husband's. Anna May couldn't remember her father ever being mean. He just went away when he drank. Not like his daughter who'd fight anything in her way when she was drunk. The bottle bounced beside her as she drove.

Anna May drove and her eyes began to see the colors of the trees. They looked like they were on fire, the reds and oranges competing with the yellows and golds. She smoked her cigarettes, drank from the thermos, and remembered this was her favorite season. She and Catherine would be cleaning the garden, harvesting the beets, turnips, and cabbage. They would be digging up the gladioli and letting them dry before packing the bulbs away. They would be planting more tulips. Catherine could never get enough tulips. It was because they had met in the spring, Catherine always said. "We met in the spring, and the tulips were blooming in that little park. You looked so beautiful against the tulips, Simon on your lap. I knew I loved you." Last autumn Simon had been five and had raked leaves and dug holes for the tulip bulbs. Catherine had made cocoa and cinnamon toast, and Simon had declared that he liked cinnamon toast better than pie.

Anna May tasted the tears on her lips. She licked the wet salt, imagining it was sweet wine on her tongue. "It's my fault," she said out loud. She thought of all the things she should have done to prevent Simon's leaving. She should have placated Tony; she should have lived alone; she should have pretended to be straight; she should have never become an alcoholic; she should have never loved; she should have never been born. Let go! she cried somewhere inside her. "Let go!" she cried aloud. Isn't that what she learned? But how could she let go of Simon and the hate she held for Tony and herself? How could she let go of that? If she let go, she'd have to forgive—the forgiveness Tony begged of her now that Simon was gone.

Even Catherine, even the woman she loved, asked her to forgive Tony. "It could have happened when he was with us," Catherine cried at her. "Forgive him, then you can forgive yourself." But Catherine didn't know what it was to feel the baby inside her, to feel him pushing his way out of her, to feel his mouth on her breast, to feel the sharp pain in her womb every time his name was spoken. Forgiveness was for people who could afford it. Anna May was poverty-struck.

The highway turned into a road, the trees crowding in on both sides of her, the flames of the trees almost blinding her. She was entering the Bruce Peninsula a sign informed her. She pulled off the road, consulting her map. Yes, she would drive to the very tip of the peninsula and it would be there she'd open the bottle and drink her way to whatever she imagined was waiting for her. The bottle rested beside her, and she touched the brown paper, feeling soothed, feeling a hunger in her stomach.

She saw another sign: Sauble Falls. Anna May thought this would be a good place to stop, to drink the last of her coffee, to smoke another cigarette. She pulled over onto the gravel lot. There was a small path leading down to the rocks. Another sign: Absolutely No Fishing. Watch Your Step. Rocks Are Slippery. She could hear the water before she saw it.

She stepped out of the covering of trees and onto the rock shelf. The falls were narrow, spilling out in various layers of rock. She could see the beginnings of Lake Huron below her. She could see movement in the water coming away from the lake and moving toward the rocks and the falls. Fish tails flashing and catching light from the sun. Hundreds of fish tails moving upstream. She walked across a flat slab of rock and there, beneath her in the shallow water, saw salmon slowly moving their bodies, their gills expanding and closing as they rested. She looked up to another rock slab and saw a dozen fish congregating at the bottom of a water spill—waiting. Her mind barely grasped the fact that the fish were migrating, swimming upstream, when a salmon leapt and hurled itself over the rushing water above. Anna May stepped up to a different ledge and watched the salmon's companions waiting their turn to jump the flowing water and reach the next plateau.

She looked down toward the mouth of the lake. There were others, like her, standing and silently watching the struggle of the fish. No one spoke, as if to speak would be blasphemous in the presence of this. She looked again into the water, the fish crowding each resting place before resuming the leaps and the jumps. Here and there on the rocks, dead fish, a testimony to the long and desperate struggle that had taken place. They lay, eyes glazed, sides open and bleeding, food for the gulls that hovered over Anna May's head.

Another salmon jumped, its flesh torn and gaping, its body spinning until it made it over the fall. Another one, the dorsal fin torn, leapt and was washed back by the power of the water. Anna May watched the fish rest, its open mouth like another wound. The fish was large, the dark body undulating in the water. She saw it begin a movement of tail. Churning the water, it shot into the air, twisting its body, shaking and spinning. She saw the underbelly, pale yellow and bleeding from the battering against the rocks, the water. He made it! Anna May wanted to clap, to shout with elation at the sheer power of such a thing happening before her.

She looked around again. The other people were gone. She was alone with the fish, the only sound besides the water was her breath against the air. She walked further upstream, her sneaker getting wet from the splashing of the salmon. She didn't feel the wet, she only waited and watched for the salmon to move. She had no idea of time, of how long she stood waiting for the movement, waiting for the jumps, the leaps, the flight. Anna May watched for Torn Fin, wanting to see him move against the current in his phenomenal swim of faith.

Anna May reached a small dam, the last barrier before the calm water and blessed rest. She sat on a rock, her heart beating fast, the adrenalin pouring through her at each leap and twist of the salmon. There he was, Torn Fin, his final jump before him. She watched, then closed her eyes, almost ashamed to be a spectator at this act, this primal movement to the place of all beginning. He had to get there, to push his bleeding body forward, believing in his magic to get him there. Believing, believing he would get there. No thoughts of death, of food, of rest. No thoughts but the great urging and wanting to get there, get *there*.

Anna May opened her eyes and saw him, another jump before being pushed back. She held her hands together, her body willing Torn Fin to move, to push, to jump, to fly! Her body rocked forward and back, her heart madly beating inside her chest. She rocked, she shouted, "Make it, damn it, make it!" Torn Fin waited at the dam. Anna May rocked and held her hands tight, her fingers twisting together, nails scratching her palms. She rocked. She whispered, "Simon. Simon." She rocked and whispered the name of her son into the water, "Simon. Simon." Like a chant. *Simon. Simon. Simon.* Into the water, as if the very name of her son was magic and could move the salmon to his final place. She rocked. She chanted. *Simon. Simon.* Anna May rocked and put her hands in the water, wanting to lift the fish over the dam and to life. As the thought flickered through her brain, Torn Fin slapped his tail against the water and jumped. He battled with the current. He twisted and arced into the air, his great mouth gaping and gasping, his wounds standing out in relief against his body, his fin discolored and shredded. With a push, a great push, he turned a complete circle and made it over the dam.

*"Simon!"* Torn Fin slapped his tail one last time and was gone, the dark body swimming home. She thought. . . she thought she saw her son's face, his black hair streaming behind him, a look of

joy transfixed on his little face before the image disappeared.

Anna May stood on the rock shelf, hands limp at her sides, watching the water, watching the salmon, watching. She watched as the sun fell behind the lake and night came closer to her. Then she walked up the path and back to her car. She looked at the bottle sitting next to her, the brown paper rustling as she put the car in gear. She drove south, stopping at a telephone booth.

She could still hear the water in her ears.

## Other titles from Firebrand Books include:

*Artemis In Echo Park*, Poetry by Eloise Klein Healy/$8.95

*Beneath My Heart*, Poetry by Janice Gould/$8.95

*The Big Mama Stories* by Shay Youngblood/$8.95

*A Burst Of Light*, Essays by Audre Lorde/$7.95

*Crime Against Nature*, Poetry by Minnie Bruce Pratt/$8.95

*Diamonds Are A Dyke's Best Friend* by Yvonne Zipter/$9.95

*Dykes To Watch Out For*, Cartoons by Alison Bechdel/$6.95

*Exile In The Promised Land*, A Memoir by Marcia Freedman/$8.95

*Eye Of A Hurricane*, Stories by Ruthann Robson/$8.95

*The Fires Of Bride*, A Novel by Ellen Galford/$8.95

*A Gathering Of Spirit*, A Collection by North American Indian Women edited by Beth Brant *(Degonwadonti)*/$9.95

*Getting Home Alive* by Aurora Levins Morales and Rosario Morales /$8.95

*The Gilda Stories*, A Novel by Jewelle Gomez/$9.95

*Good Enough To Eat*, A Novel by Lesléa Newman/$8.95

*Humid Pitch*, Narrative Poetry by Cheryl Clarke/$8.95

*Jewish Women's Call For Peace* edited by Rita Falbel, Irena Klepfisz, and Donna Nevel/$4.95

*Jonestown & Other Madness*, Poetry by Pat Parker/$7.95

*Just Say Yes*, A Novel by Judith McDaniel/$8.95

*The Land Of Look Behind*, Prose and Poetry by Michelle Cliff/$6.95

*A Letter To Harvey Milk*, Short Stories by Lesléa Newman/$8.95

*Letting In The Night*, A Novel by Joan Lindau/$8.95

*Living As A Lesbian*, Poetry by Cheryl Clarke/$7.95

*Making It*, A Woman's Guide to Sex in the Age of AIDS by Cindy Patton and Janis Kelly/$4.95

*Metamorphosis, Reflections On Recovery*, by Judith McDaniel/$7.95

*Mohawk Trail* by Beth Brant *(Degonwadonti)*/$7.95

*Moll Cutpurse*, A Novel by Ellen Galford/$7.95

*More Dykes To Watch Out For*, Cartoons by Alison Bechdel/$7.95

*The Monarchs Are Flying*, A Novel by Marion Foster/$8.95

*Movement In Black*, Poetry by Pat Parker/$8.95

*My Mama's Dead Squirrel*, Lesbian Essays on Southern Culture by Mab Segrest/$8.95

*New, Improved! Dykes To Watch Out For*, Cartoons by Alison Bechdel/$7.95

*The Other Sappho*, A Novel by Ellen Frye/$8.95

*Politics Of The Heart*, A Lesbian Parenting Anthology edited by Sandra Pollack and Jeanne Vaughn/$11.95

*Presenting... Sister NoBlues* by Hattie Gossett/$8.95

*A Restricted Country* by Joan Nestle/$8.95

*Sacred Space* by Geraldine Hatch Hanon/$9.95

*Sanctuary, A Journey* by Judith McDaniel/$7.95

*Sans Souci*, And Other Stories by Dionne Brand/$8.95

*Scuttlebutt*, A Novel by Jana Williams/$8.95

*Shoulders*, A Novel by Georgia Cotrell/$8.95

*Simple Songs*, Stories by Vickie Sears/$8.95

*The Sun Is Not Merciful*, Short Stories by Anna Lee Walters/$7.95

*Tender Warriors*, A Novel by Rachel Guido deVries/$8.95

*This Is About Incest* by Margaret Randall/$7.95

*The Threshing Floor*, Short Stories by Barbara Burford/$7.95

*Trash*, Stories by Dorothy Allison/$8.95

*The Women Who Hate Me*, Poetry by Dorothy Allison/$8.95

*Words To The Wise*, A Writer's Guide to Feminist and Lesbian Periodicals & Publishers by Andrea Fleck Clardy/$4.95

*Yours In Struggle*, Three Feminist Perspectives on Anti-Semitism and Racism by Elly Bulkin, Minnie Bruce Pratt, and Barbara Smith/$8.95

You can buy Firebrand titles at your bookstore, or order them directly from the publisher (141 The Commons, Ithaca, New York 14850, 607-272-0000).

Please include $2.00 shipping for the first book and $.50 for each additional book.

A free catalog is available on request.